CW00486245

Titchfield
A Place in History

Dedicated to the memory of
Chris Draper
Local historian and archaeologist
1917-1982

The Titchfield History Society

Titchfield
A Place in History

Edited for the
Titchfield History Society
by
Richard Wade and George Watts

Contributors: P. R. Catcheside, Trevor Cox, C. K. Currie, Keith Dingle, Michael Hare, Keith Hayward, Rosemary Hewitt, Deborah Hodson, W. J. Shaw, D.G. Smith, Arthur Tamkin, Richard Wade, Veronica Ward, George Watts, May Watts, Tom Welsh

Photographs: Keith Dingle
Drawings: Vernon Belding

First published in 1989 by
Ensign Publications
A division of Hampshire Books Ltd
2 Redcar Street
Southampton SO1 5LL

ISBN 1 85455 029 2 (Cased)
ISBN 1 85455 030 6 (Paperback)

Contents

Introduction 6
The Sarsen Stones 7
Prehistoric Sites 8
Titchfield before the Abbey 10
The Pageham Monument 13
Titchfield Abbey Library 17
Old Fishponds in the Titchfield Area 22
The Titchfield Gun 29
The Third Earl and William Shakespeare 32
Whiteley in 1594 36
The Fourth Earl and Charles I 38
The Population of Titchfield in the 16th and 17th centuries 42
The Titchfield Chain 50
A Place House Inventory: 1699 51
The Bones in the Wall 55
Some Parish Records 56
The Missing Family 65
Place House in 1737 69
Edward Ives 74
Crime and Punishment 1700-1850 76
Hubbards Mill and its Tenants 79
Titchfield 1809-1845 80
General E. C. A. Gordon 84
Changing Times 85
Sir Stephen Glynne's Description of Titchfield Church 87
Rev. G. W. W. Minns 95
The Hewett Family of Titchfield 96
Frederick Bunney 100
The Parish Council 103
A Titchfield Girlhood 108
Titchfield Charities: Titchfield Welfare Trust 112
The Ancient Parish in the 1980s 121
Further Reading 123
Acknowledgements 124
Index

Introduction

This is the second volume on the history of Titchfield to be produced by the Titchfield History Society. The success of our first volume — *Titchfield: A History*, published in 1982 — reflected the growing interest in the history of this ancient community. The present volume consists of a completely new selection of articles, items and pictures, arranged roughly chronologically, in the same popular format. As with the first volume, we do not present this as a piece of academic history: as we said then, it is an attempt to introduce a wider public to the main themes in the history of the village, and to guide those who would like to enquire further. In response to comments, however, we have this time given for each item an author's name and a brief reference to the source of the material so that students can more easily take their enquiries further. There is also an index and a note on further reading. As in the first volume, we have taken subjects from the whole area of the ancient parish of Titchfield, which stretched from Curbridge to Warsash and from Funtley to Lee-on-the-Solent.

Harry Childs looking after the churchyard.

The Sarsen Stones, West Street.

THE SARSEN STONES

The three sarsen stones which stand in the small open space half-way up West Street take the story of Titchfield back beyond history into the geological past. The sarsens are of the same material as the great stones at Stonehenge, at Avebury and other prehistoriic sites. But the Titchfield stones were not used by prehistoric man. These stones were unearthed in the 1980s near Kites Croft when the new Warsash road was being built over the stream called the Brownwich Brook. Sarsens are natural sandstone blocks about 70,000,000 years old, formed in the sandy beds which lie under the gravel top-soils of most of Titchfield Common. Where the sea washes against the gravel and the sand of the low cliff which lines the beach between Meon and Brownwich sarsen blocks from time to time fall out of the cliff face. Sarsens have also come to light throughout history when watercourses or ponds have been dug out: but the original blocks have usually been broken into smaller pieces and incorporated into ancient walls and buildings. Because stone is a rare commodity over much of southern England, medieval people thought of the blocks as strangers or foreigners — and so called them 'saracens'. The stone is raw and reddish when first dug up, but in a few years weathers into an attractive soft grey.

The three Titchfield stones, weighing between half a ton and two tons, were brought from Kites Croft by the efforts of members of the Titchfield Village Trust and with the help of Raychem, the owners of Kites Croft. Standing as they now do near the heart of this ancient village, they serve to remind us of the natural foundations on which human history has been built.

Trevor Cox

PREHISTORIC SITES

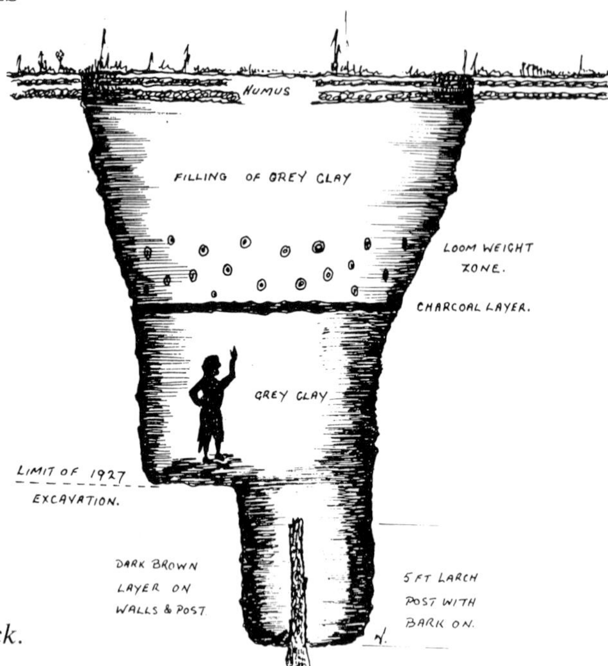

Ritual Pit at Swanwick.

The two most interesting prehistoric sites within the boundaries of the old parish of Titchfield were both in the west of the parish, along the river Hamble. Although both have been destroyed, one by gravel-digging and the other by clay-digging, they were excavated and examined just in time, by experienced archaeologists whose reports provide us with fascinating details of life in the district 3000 years ago.

Just north of the present Hook village, under the grass of Hook recreation ground, were a Late Bronze Age enclosure (about 700 B.C.) and close by a bigger Iron Age enclosure (perhaps 250 B.C. onwards) which remained in occupation in Roman times, and seems to have been reoccupied in the Middle Ages. Both settlements have been excavated and described by Dr. Paul Ashbee. Pottery from the Iron Age site suggested contacts with St. Catherine's Hill and Worthy Down. Among many interesting finds from the site were the teeth of a pony, the first known horse in the district; parts of an amphora of continental origin, almost certainly used to import wine; and iron slag, waste from the forging of semi-finished iron. A number of baked clay objects which might be weights from a weaving loom may give a connection with the ritual site at Swanwick.

The remarkable ritual pit on the Bursledon Brick Company's land at Swanwick was uncovered and later destroyed in 1927 and 1928. The first finds near the site were four of the bronze axes called palstaves found in a hole three feet deep in June 1927. Further clay-digging in October that year cut through the top section of a bigger pit to a depth of 17 feet. The pit, of grey infilling in the red clay, contained a charcoal layer above which were many baked clay objects and a quern fragment. Archaeologist Charles Fox identified the clay objects as loom weights, and dated the pit to the Late Bronze Age and Early Iron Age (1000–600 B.C.). In the following July a further level of clay was extracted, revealing that the prehistoric pit went down to 24 feet. Fox now found yet more dramatic features at the site. He found what might be described as a totem pole, a wooden post five feet high, erected in the bottom of the pit. The filling around this post, according to the workmen "stank enough to knock you down" when they cut into it. Fox believed that the filling suggested "the successive burning of such matter as blood on the sides of the pit". Anne Ross and Stuart Piggott have since identified the site as a ritual pit of the La Tène phase of Celtic culture, one of only twelve in Britain and with parallels in Germany. It is the most interesting site of its kind in Hampshire.

REFERENCES:

Charles F. Fox, "A Bronze Age Refuse Pit at Swanwick, Hants", *Antiquaries Journal* VIII, pp. 331–36 (1928)

Charles F. Fox, "The Bronze Age Pit at Swanwick, Hants: further finds", *Antiquaries Journal* X, pp. 30–33 (1930)

Anne Ross, *Pagan Celtic Britain,* 1974 edn., pp. 51–53

George Watts

TITCHFIELD BEFORE THE ABBEY

Titchfield was a royal manor in the Anglo-Saxon period, but soon after the Norman Conquest, William Rufus granted the estate to a Norman nobleman, Payn de Gisors. A century later, Payn's descendant John de Gisors rebelled against Richard the Lionheart and was expelled.

After his expulsion in 1194, Titchfield was once more a royal estate and remained so for nearly four decades, until the founding of the Abbey in 1232. Under Richard and John it was administered by local officials. Early in the reign of Henry III it was divided between two knights, and on Henry's coming of age it was briefly given to one of his closest counsellors, before being leased to an official at Portchester. This lease was ended prematurely and the land granted to the Bishop of Winchester for the construction of a Premonstratensian Abbey.

This unsettled picture may well reflect its association with the rebel Norman, John de Gisors, who continued to prosper as a vassal of the King of France until his death in 1220. Portsmouth, which de Gisors founded, was developed by King Richard, but apparently neglected by King John. Titchfield, as John de Gisors' earlier port, may have been seen as vulnerable to French attacks. Certainly, Titchfield seems to have been attached to Portsmouth in its administration and it would not be surprising if it was viewed as a political "hot potato". The stigma of John de Gisors' treachery might well have lingered for decades.

During the last four years of Richard's reign Titchfield yielded an annual income of £14 to the Treasury, but there are several references to rents and debts on the estate which suggest that there were tenants. The abbreviated Pipe Rolls do not allow distinction between officials and land holders, and it may be sufficient to list names associated with Titchfield: Henry de Stokes, Walter de Andeli, Gervase de Hawton, Gosceline de Gant, and finally in 1198, the year before Richard's death, Stephen de Turnham. Stephen appears to have been an official in Portsmouth whose name is identified with the annual returns from Titchfield in the early part of the reign of King John. By 1204 Titchfield's payments had risen to £39, perhaps reflecting the climate of inflation (Stephen paid £18 in 1208, possibly for a half-year).

According to the descent of the manor of Titchfield compiled in 1272, after the forfeiture of John de Gisors, the manor was given to Robert de Vispont. This transaction is recorded in a charter in 1219 which distinguishes the Hundred of Titchfield from the manorial lands. Titchfield, which thus had belonged to a Norman, was divided between Robert de Vispont, whose portion was valued at £15, and Milo de Beauchamp, who held 100 shillings worth. Elsewhere in Titchfield

Hundred William de Falaise was given Rowner, for services in Winchester Castle in time of war.

The next holder of Titchfield according to the 1272 document was Hubert de Burgh. His possession was brief. He resigned the estate within a few months in exchange for other lands. Until 1226 Peter de Roches, Bishop of Winchester, had been Henry III's guardian and chief minister. In that year shortly before the King attained the age of majority, Hubert de Burgh seized the Regency and forced Peter de Roches to flee to Holland. Hubert de Burgh was a powerful figure in the time of King John, serving as Justiciar, and taking a major role in the defence of John's castles against the nobles who rebelled after Magna Carta. His influence was only slighty reduced in February 1227 when Henry, aged 20, was deemed to be at the legal age of kingship. In 1228 Henry granted Titchfield to Hubert, but by the following year it was once more in the King's hands. A number of charters appear in this year. Legislation was passed bringing dire consequences on anyone who harmed the rabbits, hares or other animals in the King's warren at Titchfield. There is a grant of 23s. 5d. to the poor of Titchfield and a relief from the duties imposed by Hubert de Burgh.

Some time before the end of 1229 the Manor of Titchfield was leased to Geoffrey de Lucy, to be held at the call of the King for ten years, for a single payment of £60. Geoffrey appears to have been custodian of Portchester Castle and Guardian of the Forest of Bere. There is a record of money paid to him for his costs in employing men to repair the castle and adjoining houses. It is possible that he was a kinsman of Godfrey de Lucy, Bishop of Winchester from 1189 to 1204.

Geoffrey did not manage to keep Titchfield for the ten years allotted to him. In 1231 Peter de Roches returned from exile and was once more able to influence the King. Titchfield, as a tenanted Royal estate, was readily available for more beneficial service, to God if not to the Crown. It was therefore proposed to use the land for a religious foundation. Geoffrey was given a discharge of his holding of Titchfield with compensation of £16. In the following year authority was granted to build a Premonstratensian Abbey in honour of St. Mary. Titchfield Abbey was begun.

A few other events at the time are worthy of mention. On 13th March 1231 the Bishop of Winchester, with the King's consent, appointed John de Stowe to the church of Titchfield, the earliest recorded minister. Following the establishment of the Abbey there was a grant to the first Abbot of liberty and peace in the lands of Titchfield, but it may not have been as certain a liberty, for in 1234 the manor was exempted from taxation because it had been a gift to the Abbey. Nor was it a peaceful time to build. Hostilities with France left Titchfield vulnerable to invasion. The Abbot was obliged to supply men for the maintenance of Portchester in readiness either for attack or its use in embarking or landing troops. In 1234 the church there was damaged and the Constable of Portchester was ordered to supply timber for repair from the Forest of Bere. A similar order appears two years later.

REFERENCES:

Pipe Rolls: 7Rich I; 8Rich I; 10Rich I; 2John; 3John; 4John p.72; 6John p.122; *Close Rolls:* 1227-31, 1231-34, 1234-37; *Patent Rolls:* 1225-32; *Liberate Rolls:* 1226-40; *Charter Rolls:* vol I; British Library: Add Mss 33284; *Book of Fees* (1920 edition): vol II; *Rotulus Cancellari,* P.R.O. 1833.

Tom Welsh

THE PAGEHAM MONUMENT

Near the east window in the South Chapel of Titchfield Church is a slab of grey Purbeck marble about 7 feet long, 3 feet 3 inches broad, broken in four pieces and plastered together, with one corner cut or broken away and filled with plaster and much of its surface badly eroded. It bears the figure of a knight, his hands apparently joined in prayer. He is depicted in a mail coif, with skull cap (cerveliere) of plate worn beneath it, a mail shirt (hauberk) over which is worn a long linen surcoat; mail chausses, pryck spurs, long sword and belt originally ornamented with inlaid roundels. On his left arm he carries a shield charged with fleur-de-lys, while under his feet is a lion. Two distinct methods have been employed to produce this figure. The mail, and also apparently the shield, have been incised in the stone, while the surcoat is represented by an exactly opposite process; the lines, instead of being engraved, are left standing level with the surface of the slab. The whole of the remainder is then hollowed out to a depth of about a sixteenth of an inch and roughened to hold some sort of filling: presumably cement or plaster of Paris since there is no sign of the dowel pins, nor of pin-holes which would have been needed if brass had been used for the purpose. Similar treatment has been applied to the lion's face (the rest of him is incised) and parts of the sword (the pommel, quillons, and the decoration and chape of the scabbard).

The figure is placed beneath a straight-sided canopy of Early Decorated type, cusped and crocketed, with side shafts each engraved with part of a Latin inscription in Lombardics. This seems to begin near the top on the dexter side of the slab, continuing round the edges to finish part way up the dexter side. Unfortunately much of it is broken beyond recovery, but a combination of an earlier reading with what can now be described yields the following:-

.....SET TV DOM(INE)...(SVCCVR) RI E...AIUS...DEVS MIS (E) RERE ME...

A second inscription, in Norman-French, begins under the sinister side of the arch of the canopy, running down parallel to and inside the sinister shaft, and then vertically down, parallel to and inside the dexter shaft. It is interrupted on the sinister side by the shield, and on the dexter side by the lion's head and reads:-

WILLIAM DE PAGHE(HA)M G(I)S(T) (I)C(I) (DEV DE) SA ALME EYT MERCI

The Pageham Monument in Titchfield Church.

The surname is particularly difficult to read but intensive study during 1986 by a member of the Hampshire Genealogical Society produced a recognisable name: the first five letters and the last were recovered from the stone and were then checked against the Victoria County History and the printed Calendars. An inquisition post-mortem was held in 1305 on the death of William de Pageham who had held *inter alia* the manor of Little Funtley, a place which was then and remains in Titchfield parish.

The arms on the shield are those of the Aguillon family, an apparent contradiction. The remains of the incised letters of the surname, however, are not reconcilable with the name Aguillon. In the Parliamentary writs it is recorded that in 1282 a William de Pageham acknowledged military service due from Robert de Aguillon, who could not respond in person, being then abroad. If this William de Pageham is the one on the Titchfield monument, this service might well account for the presence of the Aguillon arms on his shield.

The slab was rediscovered in 1950 during restoration work in the South Chapel, but had been previously described in 1719. The sketch from which the inscriptions have been partly reconstructed was made then and is in the British Library. The letters in brackets were taken from that sketch.

In the absence of a legible date on the monument, conclusive proof that the subject is the William de Pageham of Little Funtley who died in 1305 is lacking. However, such circumstantial evidence as exists is consistent with that identification, and the style of the monument seems right for the period.

The Pageham family is one of a number of that name who flash in and out of the Public Records with disconcerting irregularity during the 13th and 14th centuries and then disappear completely. At various times the family held property in both Hampshire and Sussex, performed military service and carried out other official duties. Available information, although sketchy, is enough to form at least some idea of their history.

The earliest William de Pageham known to be linked with Funtley acquired property there on his marriage to Joan, daughter of Hugh de St Martin. He was temporarily dispossessed for being on the wrong side at the siege of Pevensey. It is unclear whether he was the William de Pageham who went on the 1270 crusade: if so, it is most unlikely that he came back as the expedition was decimated by disease at Tunis.

His son, also William, answered in 1282 to a summons to military service on behalf of a Robert de Aguillon who was abroad at the time and therefore unable to answer in person; one of several recorded links between the two families. From 1294 to 1301 he appears variously as performing military service, as Assessor of Subsidy, Justice of gaol delivery and Sheriff of Sussex: when he died in 1305 there was a dispute over his property. Henry of Glastonbury, as overlord, tried to repossess it over the head of the 16-year-old heir John, but custody of both heir and lands was granted to the King's daughter Mary during John's minority.

Any date which may once have been given in the inscription on the slab has eroded beyond recovery, and must therefore be inferred. However, the combination of the arms and the overall style of the slab suggest the William who died in 1305 as the more likely subject. The slab would appear to predate the construction of the South Chapel, but its original location is unknown.

By 1338, John de Pageham seems to have already died, as his daughter Mary is named as plaintiff in a suit concerning the property in Funtley. Soon afterwards she granted it to the Abbot and Convent of Titchfield. They held it until the Dissolution, when it passed to the Earl of Southampton.

REFERENCE:

British Library Add. MSS. 14296; Calendars of Patent Rolls, Close Rolls, Inquisitions Post Mortem, Fine Rolls, Inquisitions Miscellaneous; MS notes by F.A. Greenhill.

Keith Hayward

TITCHFIELD ABBEY LIBRARY

The original library of Titchfield Abbey would have consisted of its service books, scriptures and possibly some donations made on its foundation in 1232. In time this would have been added to by the labours of the canons themselves, devotional works being borrowed from other convents and copied by them. In common with other monastic orders, the Premonstratensian Canons had to carry out a certain amount of spiritual reading. The Cluniac rule laid this down as at least one volume per year, which had to be exchanged, in full view of the Chapter, on the first Monday in Lent. More frequent exchange of books was encouraged, and periods were set aside for both communal and individual reading. At first these books would be kept, together with the service books, in the church itself, or possibly in a chest in the cloister and would be under the supervision of the choirmaster or "precentor". Later the Premonstratensian Rule stated that the office of the Librarian was bound by the rule to provide for both lending and borrowing of books and was specifically enjoined to pay attention to theology, philosophy and "Literas humaniores".

By the mid-fourteenth century some monasteries had built up fair collections of books, both through their own copying and through the increasing practice of obtaining books written by professional scribes. Durham Abbey had as many as 3,000 volumes. Moreover, library science had progressed correspondingly. Not only did individual monasteries catalogue their books, but a union list of the monastic libraries of East Anglia had been compiled.

Titchfield's collection was catalogued in 1400 and it is through the catalogue, one of the finest surviving examples of a monastic catalogue, that we know about the Abbey's books. It seems likely that the library room had been built by this time, as the catalogue describes the bookcases as being "two on the Eastern face, on the Southern face the third, and on the Northern face the fourth". This would accord with the room identified as the library in the published plan, which had its entrance in the western side. This room opens from the cloister and immediately adjoins the chapter house - a typical situation for the library room. It was approximately ten feet wide and twenty-five feet long, which would be a generous allowance for a mere book room. Perhaps it was also used as a scriptorium in cold weather.

Books would be read either in the cloister, or in the monk's own cell. The catalogue (which is in the Portland collection of manuscripts on loan to the British Museum) lists a total of 326 volumes in the library for a readership of only about fourteen canons. This number must not be

A Premonstratensian Canon.

confused with books, as several books were often bound together in order to save money. Works unbound are specifically referred to in the catalogue as "in quaterno". The number of individual works listed is well over 1,000, one volume containing as many as twenty works. Titchfield's catalogue was in fact one of the earliest to list all the contents of a volume, not only the first book - a significant advance.

Another innovation in the Abbey's catalogue was the introduction which set out the arrangement of the books and gave a brief outline as to which cupboards contained which books. As stated, there were four cases, each with eight shelves. These shelves were lettered according to the class of books they had on them. Thus the shelf containing Theology, Class A, was on shelf A. This class letter might extend to several shelves if books were plentiful, as for example in class B where no less than seven shelves would have this letter. To fix the exact place of a book on the shelves, each volume was given a number with its letter class. Thus the Abbey's "Remembrance" Book (the Rememoratorium) was PX - the tenth book of class P. This identification was marked in the catalogue and on the spines and fly leaves of the books. The arrangement of the library as set out in the catalogue is briefly as follows:-

CASE 1	Shelf	1	A	Theology 4 Bibles
		2-8	B	18 Bibles with commentaries 7 commentaries on psalms
CASE 2	Shelf	1-3	C	10 commentaries on the Bible Isidore. 6 Theological vols.
		4-8	D	Gregory. 2 Theological vols. Augustine
CASE 3	Shelf	1-2	E	11 lives of saints and sermons
		3-4	F	11 canon law
		5-7	G	21 canon law commentaries
		8	H	Civil Law

CASE 4	Shelf	1	K	29 Medicine
		2	L	8 arts and 16 grammar
		3	M	
		4-5	N	20 Miscellaneous
		6	O	8 logic, 5 philosophy
		7	P	13 English Law
		8	Q	18 French volumes and 102 liturgical volumes

The books represented in the catalogue would all have been handwritten, and were nearly all in Latin. There were however a few books marked as "in anglicis", one being a rare twelfth century poem called "The Owl and the Nightingale". Printed books would have been added later in the fifteenth century. The greater part of the library consisted of religious books, but the variety of subjects represented show that the monastic idea of learning was not a narrow one. In fact monks were responsible for the saving of most of the classical literature we have, not to mention early English material and all our early history. Medicine was a particular speciality of Titchfield with 29 volumes represented. The historian R.M. Wilson remarks however that the collection would have been fifty years out of date in 1400 and probably represented the interest of one individual earlier in the century. The eighteen volumes in French remind us that the Premonstratensian Canons were a French order. Unfortunately very few volumes have survived until the present day. The dispersal in 1537 and the destruction of "Popish books" by the 1547 and 1549 Acts have done their work. Only nine volumes are listed in G.N.Ker's catalogue of surviving books, *The Mediaeval Libraries of Great Britain*. These included Richard de Glanville's *Laws of England* (Book P1) the *Magna Carta and English Statutes* (P11) and the *Remembrance Book* (PX).

The actual use of the library would have been largely confined to the fourteen or so inmates of the Abbey. However, lay persons were generally allowed to consult the books at the monastery (provided they could read Latin). Moreover, we know that sometimes books were loaned out under heavy surety to another monastery for copying, or even to a wealthy layman. The surety would have been sufficient to restrict the borrowing to the wealthiest men. There is no evidence to suggest that English convents lent freely upon a small deposit as often happened in France. Despite these restrictions on the use of their books, the monks made developments in the field of book and library science that were not surpassed until the great library awakening of the 1840s. The catalogue of Titchfield Abbey serves as a reminder of the endeavours of the monks in this as in many other fields.

REFERENCE:

Proceedings of the Hampshire Field Club, VII (1916)

P. R. Catcheside

OLD FISHPONDS IN THE TITCHFIELD AREA

Fishponds are a notable feature of the history of the Titchfield area, with much new research and fieldwork, and some important excavation having been done during the 1980s. A valuation of 1381 records six ponds on Titchfield Abbey's local lands. These are described as "within the Abbey", "on the Rector's moor", and "in the park". The map of 1610 suggests that there were two ponds lying either side of an apparent trackway in Titchfield Park near to where the present Park Farm stands. These may well be the site of the pond "in the park" mentioned in 1381. Recent fieldwork has identified two, possibly three, ponds on this site to-day. Despite evidence of more recent alterations, the upper two ponds (SU536078) seem to be original. The lower of these is equipped with a very well preserved diversion channel that would have enabled it to be drained down.

Research has shown that diversion channels and leats similar to that found near Park Farm were characteristic of many medieval ponds. Such additions not only allowed easier access to the fish; they also enabled the owner to carry out repairs more conveniently and contributed to a much more efficient system of fish husbandry. If a diversion system is available and a disease occurs in an upper pond of a series, the isolation of that disease is helped by the diversion of water around the contaminated area, thereby preventing the spread of the problem. A second advantage of diversion leats is that they allow silt brought down by a feeder stream to be taken around the ponds and not left to settle out on the pond beds. Systems without diversion facilities would quickly become choked with silt. Medieval documents show that the expense of its removal could be considerable. This expense was significantly reduced by building diversion channels. Most of the ponds associated with Titchfield Abbey seem to have been equipped with channels, although there is always the possibility that they were added by the Wriothesleys after the Dissolution.

Despite disturbances caused by the building of a new road, a diversion leat can still be identified running along the west side of Hook Pond (SU528064). There are also signs of a similar, but much mutilated, ditch on the west of another pond site to the north of Hook Pond. The earthwork dam of this pond is still extant at a point approximately SU528067, and is up to three metres high. This site has been identified as a fishpond mentioned in 1381 called "Lamberts". However, by the 18th century, this pond was referred to as Kite's Croft pond.

Diversion channels were first recognised at the ponds near the Abbey, now known as Carron Row after the small valley in which they stand.

Unfortunately evidence for their continuation along the side of the three uppermost ponds in this system was probably destroyed during its restoration in the early 1980s as a carp fishery. What appears to be the lower course of a ditch can still be seen coming around the southern end of the third dam before making its way alongside the second pond. It then empties into the lowest pond of the series, where archaeological work in 1984 uncovered a crude revetment of eight large limestone blocks.

It was originally thought that the lower pond served principally as a water reservoir for the complex system of drains under the Abbey. These were partly excavated in 1985, showing that the original medieval drain had been rebuilt at the end nearest the pond in the 16th century and again later, possibly in the 18th century. The earliest drain was found preserved under the floor of a stone building of medieval date that had once stood on the southern end of the dam. This building had at least one substantial timber supporting post internally and a thick floor of slate rubble. There were no clues to its purpose although it can be seen on the map of 1753 as still surviving, isolated from the other buildings of Place House. There is a possibility that it may have served as a storeroom of some sort. Being so close to a fishpond it is tempting to suggest that nets and other fishing equipment may have been kept there.

Since the 1985 excavations, alterations by the landowner uncovered another underground culvert leading from the upper ponds and by-passing the lowest pond. Its presence could help to explain why the lowest pond did not appear to be drainable like the other ponds in this valley. It could have allowed the lower pond to be drained by diverting water along it.

Other pond sites have been recognised within the locality. The earliest of these to have been correctly identified was at Fleet End (SU508059). Here the archaeologists, O.G.S. Crawford and Flinders Petrie recognised a massive earthwork as a fishpond dam in the 1930s. It was later confirmed as such by documentary research in the 1950s. This evidence recorded a dispute between the Abbot of Titchfield and Richard II in 1393 over a right of way that the fishpond was purported to have flooded. The case eventually found that the supposed road was not a right of way, but an illegal path that had been created since the Black Death in 1349. There is a decided hint in the documents that the fishpond at Fleet End had been created after this date.

After the dissolution of Titchfield Abbey its lands were acquired by the Wriothesleys, who showed great interest in the ponds. There is even a suggestion, in a letter of John Craiford, one of the King's Commissioners, dated January 1538, that Thomas Wriothesley considered using them for the commercial breeding of carp. If this is so, then it may be the first record of such an undertaking in this country. Contrary to popular belief English monks do not appear to have bred fish for external sale, nor is it likely that they introduced the carp to this country. Evidence to date seems to suggest the carp was a secular introduction, probably towards the end of the 14th century. Even then they do not seem to have been particularly common fish until the 16th century, and Wriothesley's interest in them in 1538 is the first time they are noted in Hampshire.

Other land acquisitions of the first Earl, made to consolidate his Titchfield estates, added to the number of ponds that had come under his control. Shortly after obtaining the Abbey estates he purchased Brownwich Manor from Sir Thomas Wyatt. This land was leased out in 1548 for three lives but the earl was specific that the lease should not include the fishing "in the pond by the manor house". This is the first reference known to "Brownwich Pond", now used by the Portsmouth Angling Club. It is much altered from its 16th century appearance by the recent inclusion of a large concrete weir in the dam. Nevertheless the pond shape seems to have little changed since it was depicted on the map of c.1610.

The carp that the Wriothesleys introduced to the Titchfield area appear to have been well established by the 18th century when there are a number of documented references to them in the ponds of the former Wriothesley estate. Clement Walcott, later to be the Duke of Portland's steward in the area, records sending specimens as gifts to the Duke's London solicitor in the 1730s and 1740s whilst correspondence continued over the division of the Wriothesley patrimony.

The division of the Titchfield estates between 1735-42 was a long and complicated affair. Walcott was particularly keen to fight the Duke of Portland's case, and in his correspondence is a wealth of detail, particularly on local topography. It is through Walcott that a previously unrecorded pond is brought to our attention. In a letter of 31st January 1742 it is noted that: "In setting off the third part of the Great Heath for my Lord Duke's Share, the great pond called New Pond falls into that of His Grace's which I know is not agreeable to Mr. Atneve, it being reputed the best Breeding Pond for Carp in all the Country".

This pond has been recognised by the large earthwork dam that spans the Fleet End stream about 500 metres above the previously mentioned Fleet End Pond. It currently stands in disused woodland (SU512061) and is one of the best preserved of the larger pond earthworks in the area. It remains a mystery as to when it was built. Walcott calls it the "New Pond", but records that it has become disused. He explains elsewhere that this is because the dam had been blown up with gunpowder some years before.

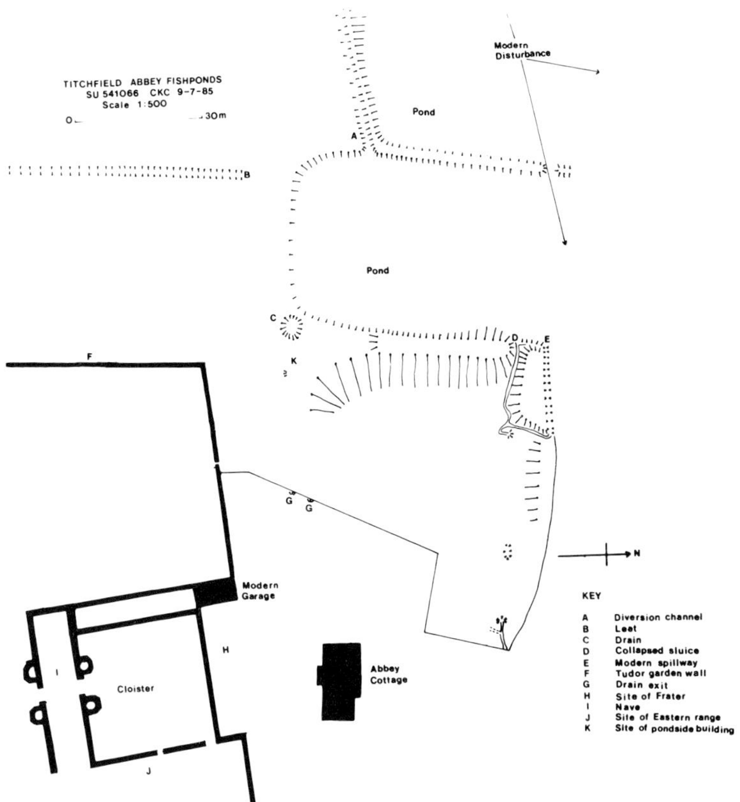

The name "New" does not help to identify its date because there are a number of medieval settlements with the prefix "New" in front of their name that are still known by that name to-day, though they could hardly be considered new in the 20th Century (the common place name "New Town" is a good example of this). It is unlikely that the pond was really "New" in 1742. The pond is probably either a late medieval or a Tudor construction.

One pond that can be fairly accurately dated is the one known as the Breach. This can still be seen on the west side of the Meon estuary at Hillhead (SU533023). It was first recorded in 1607 as a "fishery" belonging to the lord of the manor of Brownwich. Subsequent documents refer to it as a "fishpond". The Breach is unlikely to have existed much before 1607 because it is thought that the area in which it stands was reclaimed from the sea by the construction of a sea wall across the Meon estuary. This work was completed in 1611 and presumably had already begun in 1607.

The Breach is unique in that it is one of the few remaining "sea ponds" known in this country. These fisheries were constructed to supply people with fresh sea fish. They are first recorded by Roman writers such as Varro and Columella although none of this period has been recorded in Britain. The historian of Quarr Abbey has recorded a number of these ponds on the sheltered northern shore of the Isle of Wight in the medieval period, but he was unable to discover whether they were intended to hold fish caught at sea until they were required for the table, or whether they were some sort of tidal trap. Both types are known, although the former seems to have been most popular with the Romans. Such holding ponds were recorded at Warsash at the turn of the last century. Here they were used to keep fish, lobsters and crabs fresh, by local fishermen, until they were superceded by the introduction of widespread refrigeration. They are described by a local writer (F.W. Light) in 1937. He says that local tradition ascribes their original construction to the local monasteries of Hamble and Titchfield. It would be difficult to confirm such conjecture as time and tide has, quite literally washed the evidence back into the sea. Nevertheless, ponds like those described by FWL can be found in the Hamble estuary on the 25 inch O.S. map for 1909. Today yachting marinas and other modern developments cover the sites (SU489062).

The Breach, the documents of the 1740s record, was a tidal trap. Clement Walcott describes how the fishery operated in one of his many letters to the Duke of Portland's solicitor: "...when there are plenty of mullet and bass and other round fish, carp excepted, they would often come into the Breach in great sholes as there was nothing to hinder the

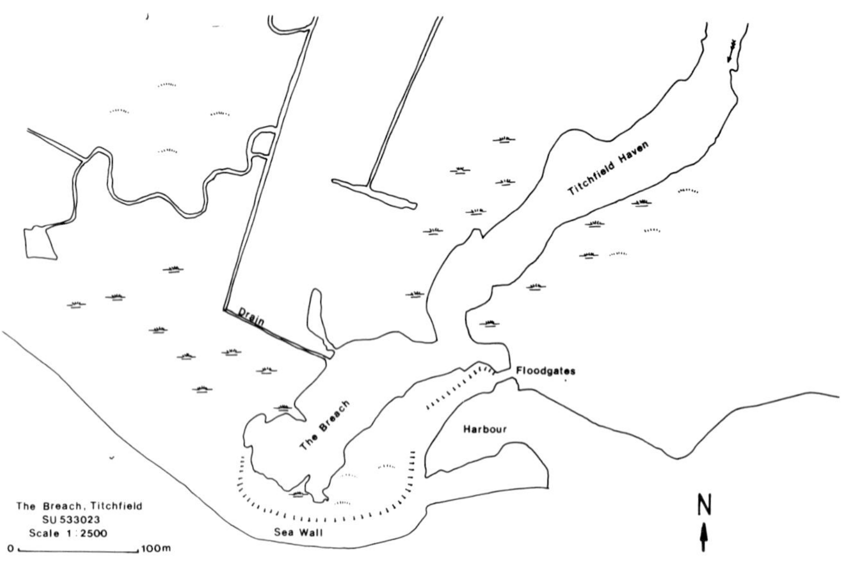

fish ...At the time when the late gamekeeper Marks was appointed .....the fishery was then worth at least £60 a year and that part of the water which now belongs to His Grace of Portland ......was worth £20 per annum, but he (Marks) made such destruction while he lived ......it is hard to catch round fish as at this time but if care is taken to encourage round fish as they used through the hatches from the sea as this was how the fishery is stocked......"

Some ponds in the Titchfield area seem to have been constructed relatively recently. One of these is the pond at Great Abshot (SU517058). But to the south-west of Great Abshot Farm is another farm known today as Solent Court (SU509050). Until the last century this farm was known as Fish House Farm and it is recorded as such in the perambulations undertaken as part of the division of the Wriothesley estates in the early 1740s. Here bounds refer to: "...Then north by fence (of) Wongars on the south and a copy estate in Titchfield called fish house on the north..."

Fish houses can be shown to have been common appurtenances to fishponds and fisheries in the past. These were thought to be places where nets, boats and other fishing equipment were stored. The abbot's fish house at Meare in Somerset, on an estate of Glastonbury Abbey, is the best known extant example. A substantial stone built one has recently been excavated in Yorkshire on the banks of a large fishpond belonging to Byland Abbey. The house recently excavated at Titchfield on the pond dam (see above) may have been a net store, and there are at least two other examples known in Hampshire.

The first of these is at Sowley Pond, where the monks of Beaulieu had a fishpond of considerable extent that still survives in use today. Here, on the tithe map, is a field adjacent to the dam known as "Fish House Croft". The other site is Fisher's Pond, near Winchester. This pond was constructed by the servants of the Bishop of Winchester early in the 13th century. By the 18th century the pond is recorded as being called Fish House Pond, and Fisher's Pond is a corruption of this name. A timber framed post-medieval building stands on the edge of the pond and this is believed to be the site of the medieval fish house.

Fish House Farm in Titchfield was not thought to have served a freshwater fishery like all the above examples, as there are no freshwater ponds sufficiently close to justify an association. The farm stands on a lane of known antiquity that leads down to the sea shore. It is therefore possible that the site once served sea fishermen working their nets and traps along the Solent shore.

The overall evidence seems to indicate that estate managers within the Titchfield area put especial store by fishing and fishponds in the past. Such a concentration of fishponds and fishery sites is not known anywhere else in Hampshire. It is unfortunate that the documentary sources are so piecemeal and that, in many cases, continued usage of these valuable resources has destroyed much of the evidence for their original layout. On top of this, survival is seriously hampered by continuing housing development and road schemes within the area. As this is being written future developments threaten a number of the sites described. Fortunately the lower dam at Carron Row was excavated just in time. It was here that constructional techniques recorded in medieval and Tudor documents relating to ponds were first confirmed by archaeological method. This excavation showed that the dam was made by ramming consecutive layers of clay, on average about 20 cms. (8 inches) thick, on top of one another. Only when each layer had been properly compacted was another added. This ensured that the dam should remain watertight; and this has been proved by the hundreds of years of continued use this pond has been put to. When workmen dug into the side of the dam of Kite's Croft Pond in 1985 to fill sandbags with ballast, they revealed an identical method of construction to that of the pond at the Abbey. Time and time again such passing indications hint at common links between the old ponds in the Titchfield area.

REFERENCES:

E. Roberts 1986: "The Bishop of Winchester's Fishponds in Hampshire 1150-1400". *The Proceedings of the Hampshire Field Club and Archaeological Society* 42, pp. 125-138

T. Welsh & C.K. Currie 1986: "Earthworks at Park Farm, Titchfield". *Hants Field Club Newsletter:*new series 6, pp.18-19

C.K. Currie 1988: "Hampshire Fishponds" in M.A.Aston ed. *Medieval Fish, Fisheries and Fishponds in England,* British Archaelogical Reports (British Series) 182, Oxford.

C.K. Currie

THE TITCHFIELD GUN

Early in 1957 a Mr J. Godden of Crescent Road, Locks Heath, was ploughing land alongside the south boundary wall of Titchfield Abbey (probably where the Garden centre is now situated), when he found a lump of metal weighing about 10lbs. Having removed some of the grime he could see it was bronze with an inscription:

ROBERT-AND-JOHN-OWEN-BRETHREN-MADE-THIS-PECE-AN-D-1537

Mr Godden took his find to the Portsmouth Museum Service where the Curator, Mr W. Corney, sent it to Mr Rigold of the Inspectorate of Ancient Monuments at the Ministry of Works for authentication. Mr Rigold replied:

"It is part of a gun and nothing to do with the Abbey which would not have a gun (I hope not, at least) while the date makes it too early for any piece made specially for Wriothesley at Place House, unless of course he brought it there. 'Pece' means a piece of ordnance. The two gunfounders are a well-known pair and they made many of the guns required for the parishes in the Isle of Wight when they were required to have one in the 1540s. Three, at least, survive".

Mr Godden's find is still in Portsmouth Museum, and as we now know many of the guns raised from the *Mary Rose* were also made by the Owen Brothers.

A history of the Oglander family at Nunwell on the Isle of Wight *(Nunwell Symphony)* may give another clue to the origin of the Titchfield Gun:

"It was quite in keeping with traditional English behaviour that, after the defeat of the French in 1545, all interest in questions of Home Defence immediately evaporated. But in the Isle of Wight four years later the principal parishes were provided with bronze canons which were trundled about on all parades and exercises. All of these guns but one have long since disappeared, but this remaining gun, which belonged to George's canton, is still looking out to sea on its old carriage at Nunwell. With its clearly legible description, "JOHN AND ROBERT OWEN BRETHREN MADE THIS PECE 1549", it can boast a notable record. Having watched the approach of the Armada in 1588 and paraded faithfully with generations of defenders through all successive alarms till the final overthrow of Napoleon, it was eventually used by the joyous inhabitants of Brading to give a *feu de joie* on the passing of the Reform Bill in 1832. But that was the

A fragment of the Titchfield Gun.

warrior's swan song. To ensure a memorable bang it was loaded up to the muzzle and the resulting jagged crack destroyed its erstwhile symmetry".

The Nunwell gun was taken to Carisbrooke Castle in the late 1950s and is still on view there. The third and fourth Earls of Southampton were in charge of the island's "Home Guard" and *Nunwell Symphony* quotes from letters written by the Earls giving instructions on the extent and frequency of the training of the Volunteers.

The finding of the gun fragment at Titchfield raises some interesting questions. Was it from a gun belonging to the Wriothesleys? Was it one of the Isle of Wight guns brought to Titchfield? Could it have been for the defence of the home of the Wriothesleys as Governors of the Isle of Wight? If the Government of the day had decided that the island should be defended, then would it have made sense to defend some of the nearest points on the mainland? We have yet to find answers.

Keith Dingle

The Nunwell Gun.

THE THIRD EARL AND WILLIAM SHAKESPEARE

In *Titchfield: A History* we talked about William Shakespeare's supposed connection with the village of Titchfield: and we dismissed the Gobbos and the Beestons as inaccuracies. In this chapter we look in more detail at his connection with the Wriothesley family of Place House. As with every other aspect of Shakespeare's life, we have remarkably little hard evidence; all one can say is that some guesses are a little more plausible than others.

Henry Wriothesley, the third Earl of Southampton, was for a time one of Shakespeare's patrons: the poems *Venus and Adonis,* published in 1593, and *The Rape of Lucrece,* published in 1594, were both dedicated to him. It has also often been supposed (on very little evidence) that the young Earl was the Fair Youth of Shakespeare's *Sonnets* and that Shakespeare also knew the Earl's mother, the dowager Countess and eligible widow whose maiden name had been Mary Browne. It has sometimes been suggested (though there is even less evidence for this) that the Countess was the Dark Lady of the *Sonnets.* Part of this argument is that the references in the sonnets to 'dark' and 'black' are elaborate puns on the Countess' maiden name.

For I have sworn thee fair, and thought thee bright
Who art as black as hell, and dark as night.

(Sonnet 147)

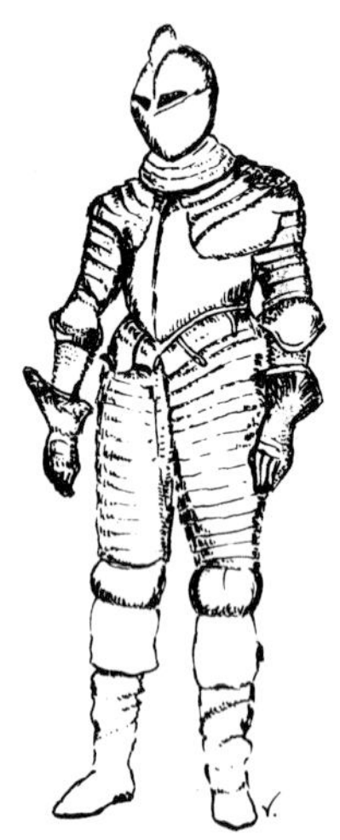

Armour of the Third Earl of Southampton.

Certainly Shakespeare, like other Elizabethan writers, was capable of making bad puns of this kind. Critics of this Browne/Dark association point to the thinly disguised and sometimes fairly gross sexuality of some of the Dark Lady passages, and to the unlikelihood of a great lady like the Countess permitting such familiarity from a commoner of humble origin, however talented. But Elizabethan and early Stuart writers and readers were accustomed to innuendoes of this kind, particularly in poems which, like Shakespeare's sonnets, were circulated in manuscript. If on those grounds, the Dark Lady could not be Mary Browne, then the Fair Youth of the Sonnets, who has an implied homosexual relationship with the poet, could not be Henry Wriothesley either; other scholars, among them the distinguished historian, Dr. A.L. Rowse, have proposed rival and plausible, candidates for the Dark Lady role.

Shakespeare did not of course need to visit Titchfield to meet the Wriothesleys. Though Place House was their family home, both the young Earl and the Countess were frequently at their London house, then in Holborn, and in and around the Court. But it does seem likely that Shakespeare visited Hampshire at least once. During the plague epidemic of 1593, Lord Strange's Company, of which Shakespeare was then a member, spent several weeks of May and June in Southampton. It would seem to be one of the more reasonable guesses about Shakespeare's movements that, in the midst of writing and publishing two long poems for his current patron, and while deterred by the epidemic from staying in London, he should have visited one or other of Wriothesley's two houses near Southampton - Titchfield and Beaulieu, perhaps to act or to read the two poems. That takes us back to the Sonnets. The Sonnets were not published until 1609, just before Shakespeare retired to live in Stratford. But it seems probable that most of them were written in the early 1590s, before being circulated in manuscript. Shakespeare, then, may well have been in South Hampshire while he was writing some of the Sonnets. So —

Thou art thy Mother's glass, and she in thee
Calls back the lovely April of her prime. *(Sonnet 3)*

Are they Wriothesley and his mother Mary Browne?

Seeking that beauteous roof to ruinate
Which to repair should be thy chief desire

(Sonnet 10)

Is this Beaulieu Abbey, which Wriothesley was rebuilding?

Like as the waves make toward the pebbled shore
So do our minutes hasten to their end

(Sonnet 60)

Mary Browne, mother of the Third Earl of Southampton.

Are we on the Solent shore?
And finally —

Let this sad int'rim like the ocean be
Which parts the shore, where two contracted new
Come daily to the banks.

(Sonnet 56)

Is this a picture of Mary Browne riding by the shore with Sir Thomas Heneage whom she was to marry as her second husband in May 1594?

The year 1594 may mark the end of the Wriothesley-Shakespeare connection. Several writers have suggested that *A Midsummer Night's Dream* was commissioned for part of the marriage celebrations of Heneage and the Countess (though it is more likely to have been staged in London than in Titchfield). But the marriage may have signalled the end of the supposed flirtation, however platonic, between the Countess and the poet. The young Earl himself came of age in Ocober 1594, and again the poet may have been amongst the childish things the great man resolved to put away (something later reflected in the relationship between Falstaff and Henry V in the plays?).

An interesting local footnote comes in the relationship of the poetic events to the construction of the magnificent Wriothesley monument in Titchfield Church. The second Earl had left money for this purpose at his death in 1581, but the contract for its erection was not signed until 1594, and we can guess that it was actually installed after the third Earl came of age in the winter of 1594-95. If Shakespeare had still been on the Earl's poetic payroll at that time, it seems inconceivable that a celebratory poem would not have been commissioned or some flattering insertion made in a sonnet or a play: but no such insertion has yet been identified. So it seems likely that Wriothesley, now flirting with ladies around the Queen's court, and increasingly caught up in the dangerous world of politics — and William Shakespeare, now a successful writer cannily investing his earnings in property in his native county — became merely distant acquaintances after 1594, a bow from the stage and a purse thrown back only reminders of a relationship now wisely half-forgotten. But Shakespeare scholarship is like a timeless Test match: it seems to go on and on, but a new idea — even a new fact — may appear at any time. There are still many archives to search.

REFERENCES:

Shakespeare's Southampton, A.L. Rowse (1965)
Shakespeare and the Earl of Southampton, G. Akrigg (1968)
Minstrels and Players in Southampton, C.E.C. Burch (1969)

Richard Wade
George Watts

WHITELEY IN 1594

Until the announcement of the Whiteley Development Plan, few had heard the name Whiteley and even fewer knew where it was — somewhere between Burridge and Titchfield Lane perhaps — a veritable no man's land, though soon to be as well known a name as Fareham or Locksheath. But some 400 years ago Whiteley had burst into (temporary) prominence through a bizarre event with far-reaching repercussions.

Two prominent Wiltshire families, the Longs and the Danvers, had been quarrelling for many years, and as a result of Sir John Danvers sending one of the Long servants for trial (he had committed robbery and murder), in 1594 feelings between the families became very bitter. This resulted in a fight between the Danvers men led by Sir John's sons, Henry and Charles, and Henry Long's gang. During the fight Henry Long drew his sword and wounded Charles Danvers and would have probably killed him had not Henry Danvers intervened, leaving Henry Long dead on the floor. Realising the position they were in, the Danvers decided to escape and mounting their horses galloped through the night, hoping to reach the coast and cross the Channel. The Danvers had been close friends of the Earl of Southampton and knew the Earl would do all he could to assist in their plan. They rode to Whiteley Lodge, then one of the Earl's farms. There the party was given food and lodging while Charles had his wound attended to.

Thomas Dymock, the tenant and one of the Earl's trusted servants, realising that instant action was essential, sent a message to the Earl at Place House telling him his friends wished to see him. On hearing the news, and in spite of being in the middle of celebrations marking his twenty-first birthday and his majority, he arranged to ride over the following afternoon, and stayed the night at Whiteley Lodge. Though the Earl was aware of the danger of helping two wanted men he took the risk. The plan was to go down to Swanwick at dawn and engage the ferrymen, William and Henry Reed, to take the party across the Solent to Calshot Castle where they could hide until another boat could get them away. Seeing the boat moving down the river, Henry must have heaved a sign of relief as he galloped back home to take his place at the centre of his festivities.

But on arrival at Calshot the fugitives were confronted with another danger. The deputy governor of the Castle refused them permission to land until he received clearance from the Castle Governor, Captain Thomas Parkinson, who lived in Southampton, 17 miles away. To allay suspicion the party was forced to cruise between Calshot and St.

Andrew's Castle near Hamble where the boat was anchored for the night. The next morning Thomas Dymock arrived with the Governor's warrant for them to land. But before they found a boat suitable, a hue and cry had been put out making a hasty retreat again imperative, for officers were on their way to apprehend them. The party sailed under cover of darkness across to Hillhead (then called Baldhead); once more, guided by Dymock, they reached Whiteley and from there moved on to Place House where they were harboured until a passage could be arranged. After three years in exile Henry and Charles Danvers were pardoned and returned to England, playing an important part in the Earl of Essex's campaigns in Ireland.

There is some uncertainty about the site of the 'sixteenth century Lodge. A house in Whiteley Lane bears the name Whiteley Lodge; parts of it are quite old with an inglenook fireplace and oak beams. But the former Whiteley Farm had a very large six-bedroomed house, with cellars said to be large enough to drive a horse and cart around. It was demolished about 1950. It is almost certain to be the house mentioned in this sixteenth century story.

REFERENCE:

Shakespeare's Southampton, A.L. Rowse, 1965

Trevor Cox

THE FOURTH EARL AND CHARLES I

Thomas Wriothesley, the fourth Earl of Southampton, was the second son of Shakespeare's patron, and succeeded to the title at the age of 17 when his father and elder brother died on campaign in the Low Countries. In his youth he was an intimate at the royal court (Charles I and his bride Henrietta Maria spent their honeymoon at Place House), but in the 1630s Wriothesley found himself in opposition to the royal government following a dispute about his property around Beaulieu. As a result, during 1640-41 he acted with the parliamentary opposition to the King, but as the quarrel became more bitter he took the royal side and became one of the King's closest advisers during the first stage of the Civil War. After the battle of Naseby he became one of the royal negotiators for peace terms, but went home to Titchfield when the King was put under surveillance in Hampton Court in November 1647.

Then there occurred one of the most dramatic incidents in the long history of Titchfield. The King feared that if he stayed in Hampton Court he would be seized by one of the extreme factions of the Parliamentary army. So he planned an escape, first to the Earl's house at Titchfield, thence by ship either to the Isle of Wight or to France. One November night in foul weather and with only three companions Charles left Hampton Court, and after losing their way in Windsor Forest reached Farnham by morning. They then rode into Hampshire intending to change their horses at the Ship Inn at Bishop's Sutton; but when they got there they found that the Parliamentary Committee for Hampshire was already meeting at the inn. The King rode on with one companion to Place House, while the others made their way to the Isle of Wight where the Governor, Colonel Hammond, was thought to be sympathetic to the King. Hammond was persuaded to come across to Titchfield with only one companion to talk to the King. On his arrival the King was alarmed. Told by his courtier, Jack Ashburnham, that Hammond was downstairs the King is reported to have said "What! Have you brought Hammond with you? Oh Jack you have undone me! — for I am by this means made fast from stirring". Ashburnham offered to go downstairs and kill Hammond and his companion but the King refused to condone a murder. As there was no news of a ship for France, Charles agreed to go with Hammond to Carisbrooke Castle. Charles believed that the inhabitants of the Isle of Wight were sympathetic to him and that the small parliamentary garrison there offered him no threat. He remained in Carisbrooke for a year, and the Fourth Earl was amongst his visitors there. But in the event Hammond kept the King effectively under house arrest; and once Parliament decided that the King was too dangerous to

Thomas Wriothesley, Fourth Earl of Southampton.

leave there, a new Governor and new troops arrived, took Charles to Hurst Castle, thence to Whitehall and his trial.

The faithful fourth Earl now joined the King in Whitehall, and remained with him during the trial. It was Wriothesley who is said to have sat through the night with the King's body after the execution, and to have been the witness of the cloaked figure of Cromwell coming into the room in the darkness and saying "Stern necessity".

The new regime was surprisingly lenient to the fourth Earl. He was fined nearly £6,500, supposedly one tenth of the value of his property, and required to pay £250 a year for the maintenance of puritan ministers in Hampshire. He spent most of this time during the Commonwealth and Protectorate period on his country estates, but his semi-retirement did not prevent him spending a great deal of money building himself a great new house, Southampton House (long since demolished) on his London property in Bloomsbury.

At the restoration of Charles II in 1660, Wriothesley rejoined the court and became Lord High Treasurer, struggling to balance Charles' budget. But he was by now a rather old fashioned man, and had no sympathy with the style of the new monarchy. He suffered from increasing illness, and gradually withdrew from active business. He died in London in May 1667 and was buried in Titchfield Church.

The fourth Earl had been a friend of the Earl of Clarendon, another of Charles II's ministers and later the historian of the period. Clarendon wrote an affectionately critical description of Wriothesley, describing him as of small stature but very brave. He often suffered from bouts of melancholy and could be very reserved with strangers, but with his friends he could be pleasant and cheerful. He was something of a snob and liked to be called 'My Lord'. In private he could be lazy, but when on business could be very energetic. At the time of the negotiations for the Treaty of Uxbridge in 1645 he slept for only four hours a night for 20 days. He was a devout Anglican, being profoundly opposed both to Puritanism and Catholicism. "There is a good man gone" said the diarist Pepys at his death.

When the fourth Earl died, without a male heir, his three daughters simply drew lots for the inheritance. Elizabeth, his eldest daughter who was married to Edward Noel, later the first Earl of Gainsborough, inherited her father's Titchfield estates including Place House. Rachel, the second daughter, inherited the London property which eventually came into the possession of the Dukes of Bedford, while the youngest daughter Elizabeth by the Earl's second marriage, acquired the Beaulieu estates which ultimately became the property of the Dukes of Montagu

Edward Noel inherited the Titchfield estates following his wife's death in 1680, and when he died in 1689 these passed to his only surviving son, Wriothesley Baptist Noel, second Earl of Gainsborough. Sadly he too died the following year aged 25, leaving a young widow Katherine and two infant children, Elizabeth and Rachel. "Wriothesley" was to disappear even as a Christian name.

Richard Wade

THE POPULATION OF TITCHFIELD IN THE 16th AND 17th CENTURIES

The Parish Registers for Titchfield do not begin until 1589-90, and so our best source for the population of the village at the beginning of the period is the 1546 Survey. This Survey was compiled by the first Earl to assess the income from his newly acquired lands in Titchfield. The date given on the Survey is 1546: but it is possible that the Survey was a revised copy of one made earlier. At the beginning of the Survey there is frequent mention of lands being granted to the tenants of the Abbey. Furthermore a number of the charters concerning land and rent are described as being deposited in the pyx (box) at Titchfield. It is possible therefore that the Survey was taken in the 1530s before or immediately after the takeover of the Abbey, and that this Survey was updated for Wriothesley's purposes in 1546.

The Survey does not give us the total population figure for Titchfield — this can only be estimated. The number of tenements listed for the town (the market square and the streets immediately adjacent) was 86. By multiplying this number by a supposed family size, the total population can be estimated. If the average family size is taken as 4.5, as the historian W.G. Hoskins suggests, the population would be 387 in the town itself. In 1377 a Survey made by the Abbot stated that 88 tenants were to be found in Titchfield: the total population at that time can therefore be calculated as 396 people. So that in almost two hundred years the population had changed little. It is also interesting to compare the population of Titchfield in 1546 with that estimated for neighbouring Fareham. Before the Black Death of 1349, Titchfield had been considered more important, and was one of the Hampshire market towns most heavily assessed for taxation in 1333. But compared to the figure of 387 for Titchfield, Fareham was, by 1600, estimated to have been one of only eight places in Hampshire to have had a population of over one thousand. It appears then that Fareham had expanded at a faster rate than Titchfield and was perhaps by 1600 more important to the local area.

Examination of the people of Titchfield listed in the 1546 Survey reveals 65 different names, with ten tenants holding 22 properties between them. This suggests that a number of the tenements were sublet: but without further evidence this is difficult to prove. One indication is given by an entry in the Survey stating that Robert Godfrey held by indenture of a lease made to Thomas Childley, a "new" tenement formerly held by John Weston. Of the ten tenants who held more than one property, five were significantly wealthier and paid considerably higher rents. For example, one of the wealthier tenants was

Swanwick and Burseldon — 1610 map.

Robert Godfrey who held the George Inn and two other properties. His rent amounted to 40s.3d. Another tenant of high standing was John Jermayne, who held four properties, with rent for three of them amounting to 30s.3d. In contrast, most tenants in Titchfield held only a tenement and garden which in a number of cases had a small amount of land attached. The average rent for these properties was 5s. (25p.), though in some cases it was as high as 12s. So in 1546 the tenants of Titchfield were mainly small property holders who lived alongside the few wealthier tenants who could afford to hold more than one property.

From 1589-90 the Parish Registers are available. These are precise in the numbers given, but not necessarily more accurate. In the period covered by this chapter they are often difficult to read. Up to 1606 they are particularly untidy, with much crossing out. Between 1606 and 1627 the condition improves and they become easier to read. But from 1627 to 1639 they are again difficult to read, and in some places the pages are torn and in pieces. It seems that for some reason the registers for this period had been copied out again, as the entries for 1634 are found after 1638. From 1638 to 1670 the registers are on the whole better kept, though some gaps do exist, particularly in the marriages section.

In the years 1590-99 a comparison of the number of baptisms over burials reveals no significant differences. There were 378 births to 374 burials overall. This suggests that at that time the population of Titchfield was stable. In the years 1600-1609 the situation was different, with the number of baptisms considerably larger than the number of burials. Compared with the previous decade, the number of baptisms has increased to 483 and the burials have declined to 346. This implies a rise in population. A possible alternative reason for fewer people dying in the village than are born there would be migration out of the village: but the difference is so marked that it is most likely that there was an actual rise in population. Using a conventional multiplier of baptisms to population of 33 would give a population estimate for the whole parish of some 1,250 in the 1590s, and 1,580 in 1600-1609.

In the years 1610-19 there was a surplus of burials over baptisms, with 475 burials to 437 baptisms. Compared to 1600-1609, the baptisms have decreased slightly while the burials have increased by 129. In the year 1612 there were 63 burials and in 1613 there were 86: both figures are considerably higher than the average for the whole decade of 47.5 deaths. On the other hand, a normal number of 86 infants were baptised in the two years, which suggest that the cause of death is unlikely to have been famine, which usually severely affects fertility. We can guess therefore that the cause of the higher mortality was an epidemic of disease, perhaps plague.

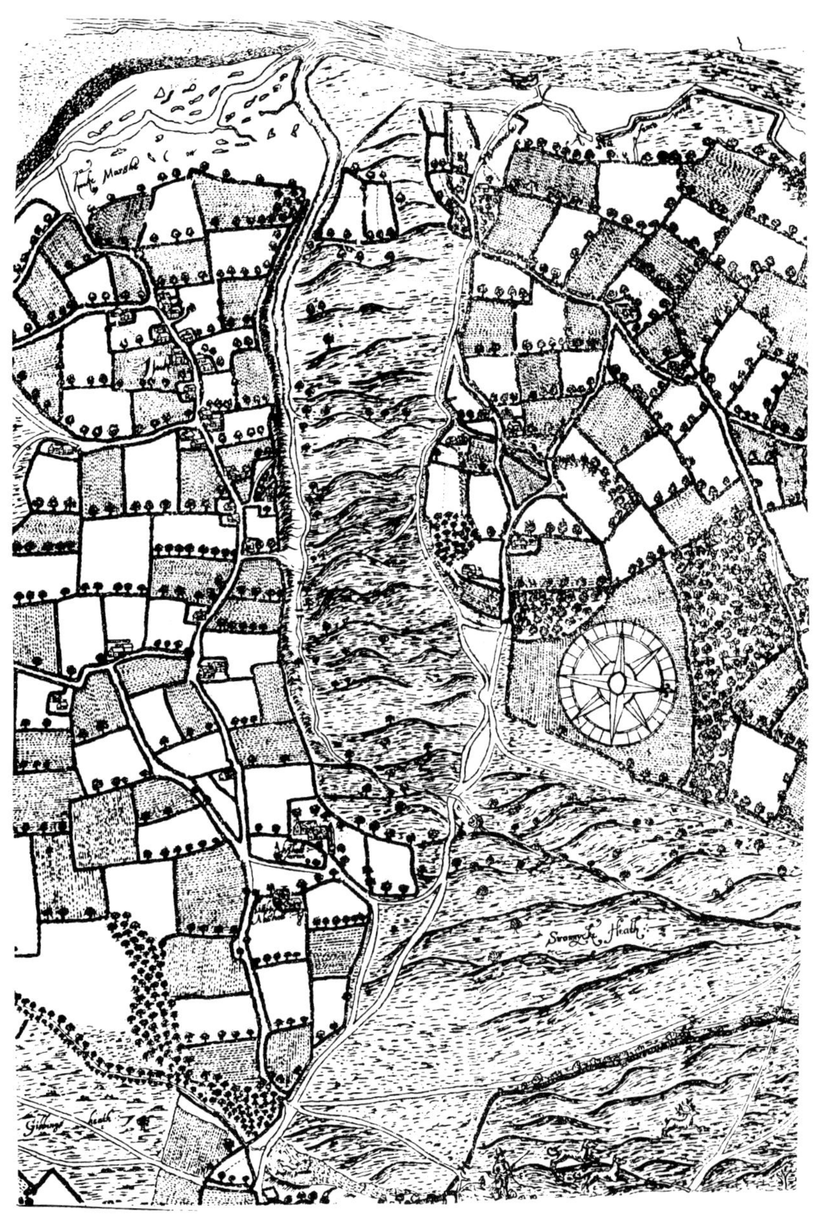

The Mouth of the River Hamble and East to Abshot — 1610 map.

In the following decade, 1620-29, there were 440 baptisms and 421 burials, which again suggests that the population was rising. The number of burials was also significantly lower than in the previous decade. But in this decade a Survey of 1624-5 provides alternative evidence with which to measure the population. This Survey is similar in layout to that of 1546. It lists 98 tenements in Titchfield itself compared to 86 in 1546 (14% more). By multiplying this figure by 4.5 the total population of the town can be estimated as 441. Since 1546 the town population would seem to have risen by 54, thus supporting the evidence from the Parish Registers of an increase in the population.

A study of the tenants themselves in this Survey once again reveals 65 actual names. Compared with 1546 when ten tenants held 22 properties, in 1625 there were eleven tenants holding 33 properties between them. The explanation for this is presumably that increased prosperity enabled some tenants to increase their wealth and landholdings. These larger landholders include Arthur Broomfield. He held four separate properties in Titchfield, plus St Margaret's just outside the town. The Wriothesley deeds show us that Arthur Broomfield was an agent employed by the earls of Southampton in connection with the Fontley Iron Mill. Another employee of the third Earl was Mr Chamberlain, who managed the iron works and was described as having land at Swanwick.

Comparison of the 1546 and 1624-5 Surveys also provides evidence of long-established families in the town. Families listed in both Surveys include the Mayle and Sabyn families, the Fosters and the Hartwells. These last two were quite wealthy. For example, Edward Hartwell held six different properties in the High Street, West Street and South Street in 1625: in 1546 the family had held only two tenements, in West Street and South Street. So between 1546 and 1625 the increasing prosperity of Titchfield had led to the establishment of various prosperous families in the town as well as a rising population.

Analysis of the Parish Registers for the years 1630-39 shows a marked surplus of baptisms over burials, with 496 baptisms and 386 burials. Compared with the previous decade the number of baptisms had increased and the number of burials has decreased, suggesting continued population growth. However, the 1632 Survey of the Titchfield Manors does not seem to support this view. It lists only 69 tenants in Titchfield compared with 98 in 1624-5. The most likely explanation for this discrepancy is that the 1632 Survey is incomplete and does not list all the tenants of the town because it was mainly concerned with assessing the value, quality and quantity of land, and did not include tenancies of people who held no land. Such people were most likely to have been

The Mouth of the River Meon — 1610 map.

found in cottages in the town, explaining the lower number of tenants in that area.

In 1640-49 there was again a surplus of baptisms over burials suggesting continued population increase. There were 563 baptisms, more than in 1630-39: however the figure for burials, 472, also increased. Together with the fact that the surplus of baptisms over burials has decreased from 110 in the years 1630-39 to 91 for the years 1640-49, this may suggest a reduction in the rate of population growth. The parish population may have peaked during that decade, at about 1800 people.

The figures for the 1650s indicate that the population was no longer increasing: in fact, a surplus of burials over baptisms suggests that it may have been decreasing. There were the same number of burials, 472, as in the preceding decade, so the mortality was not the key factor. But the number of baptisms shows a marked decline, from 563 in the 1640s to only 327 in the 1650s. We cannot tell whether this was in any way due to a change in religious practices during the Commonwealth and Protectorate period. For the 1660s the Parish Registers give us our final evidence for the condition of Titchfield under the Wriothesleys. Once again there were more burials than baptisms, 443 burials and 428 baptisms. So the population seems still to have been in decline. That the number of burials is lower than in either of the previous decades may suggest a lower population and perhaps some migration from the parish.

A new source of population data, the Hearth Tax of 1665, lists 73 different houses in Titchfield town: 18 of these posessed non-chargeable hearths associated with poverty. By multiplying 73 by 4.5 the total town population can be estimated as 328. The figure for the Earl's tenants in the 1624-5 Survey had been 441: this reduction supports the evidence of the Parish Registers for a decline in the population. Furthermore, only five people owned more than one property and the most owned by one person was three, held by George Marsh. In contrast, in 1546 ten people had held more than one property and in 1624-5 there had been eleven tenants with several properties. So there seems to have been a fall in the number of wealthy tenants. But this does not mean there were no longer any wealthy people in Titchfield in 1665, as seven people were taxed for five or more hearths. George Marsh's three properties had 29 hearths in them, so by the standards of Titchfield at the time he was quite wealthy. Further analysis of the Hearth Tax makes it possible to trace seven families back to the 1632 Survey; two of these, the Hartwells and the Sabyns, can also be traced back to 1546.

Yet another source of population data for the seventeenth century, at least for adults, are two surveys of communicants. In 1603 there were said to be 819 Anglican communicants and four recusants in Titchfield parish. By 1676 there were 869 communicants, two papists and 47 nonconformists, 918 adults in all.

So for the particular period 1665-76 we have three independent sources for the population of the whole parish — the Hearth Tax, the Parish Register and the survey of communicants. The Hearth Tax lists 308 households in the parish: multiplied by 4.5 this points to a total population of 1,376. If we multiply the annual average of baptisms (43) by the conventional 33, we get a remarkably similar figure, 1,419. Using the 1676 data, and assuming that there were as many non-communicant children as church-attending adults, we get a rather higher figure, 1,728.

The four sources for the population of Titchfield town and Titchfield parish over the whole period between 1546 and 1676 (the property surveys, the Parish Registers, the Hearth Tax, and the communicant surveys) provide us therefore with broadly consistent data. They suggest increasing population in the sixteenth century, accelerating in the early seventeenth century to a peak of about 1,800 people in the parish sometime in the 1640s. Thereafter there seems to have been a decline to perhaps 1,400 in the 1660s.

It is difficult to determine whether these population changes were due to local or national trends. The original increase may have been associated with the enthusiastic development of his estates by the third Earl of Southampton: but it is also thought that the population of the whole of England rose in those same years, perhaps doubling between 1541 and 1656. Similarly, the decline may have been a delayed-action result of the shutting-off of the Meon estuary and the failure of the third Earl's canal project, or of the local effects of fighting in the Civil War: but national historians have also identified a phase of population decline between 1656 and 1686. Whatever the factors involved, in Titchfield the period of decline seems to have continued in the early eighteenth century.

REFERENCES:

Wriothesley deeds (Hampshire Record Office)5M53/764, 767-9
Parish Registers (Hampshire Record Office)
Hearth Tax, 1665 (Titchfield History Society, 1985)
The Compton Census of 1676 ed. A Whiteman (1986).

Deborah Hodson

THE TITCHFIELD CHAIN

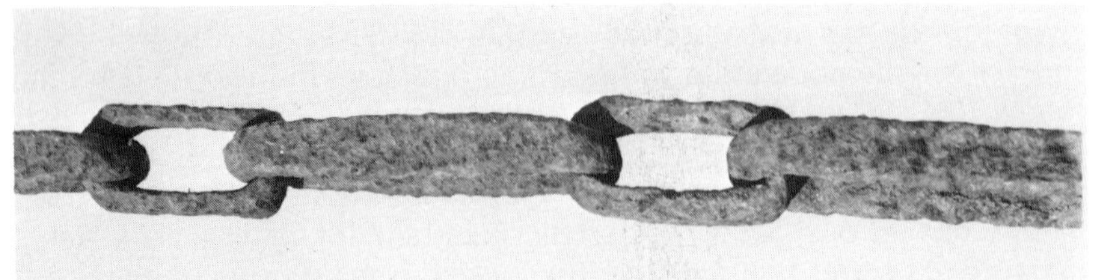

Part of the Titchfield Chain.

By the roadside just south of Segensworth House is a length of worn chain, about 10 metres long, now used as a boundary marker. The chain is unusual in consisting of alternate long and short links, each measuring six or twelve centimetres. What makes the chain interesting is that lengths of the same chain once existed in two other places on the edge of the village, one outside a house in Springles Lane off the Fontley road, and another, longer section along the side of Hollam Hill on the Crofton Road: and that there is a local tradition that the chain once stretched round the whole village. A similar chain is said to have existed at Shaftesbury in Dorset. One suggestion for the functions of such chains is that during the seventeenth century Civil War they were raised to about waist height each evening to deter groups of marauding cavalrymen from galloping into the village during the night. Quite a different suggestion is that they were wound on windlasses and used to haul heavy horse-drawn wagons up steep inclines (though the long and short links seem to make them unsuitable for that purpose). Were they part of the scrap from some naval vessel? If they were boundary markers, why did the old parish want to mark its boundaries so precisely? Perhaps the traditions of other villages can provide us with more clues to solving the mystery of the chain.

Trevor Cox

A PLACE HOUSE INVENTORY : 1699

Place House in 1720, from the North-East.

(For an enlarged version of this unique view of Place House from the North-East, see page 127).

On 12th May 1699 an inventory of some of the contents of Place House was drawn up. This followed the early death in 1690 of Wriothesley Baptist Noel, the second Earl of Gainsborough. Noel had succeeded his father in 1689, inheriting the manors of Titchfield and Place House. Noel's widow, Katherine, was left with two young daughters, Elizabeth and Rachel — and nine years later on 12th March 1699 she re-married, John Sheffield, Marquis of Normanby. The following May part of the personal estate of the late Earl was sold by Normanby to Katherine's father, Lord Brook, for the benefit of the two young daughters, co-heiresses of the Titchfield estates.

In 1699 Place House or the "Palice" as it was sometimes called comprised thirty-nine main rooms including the family's private chambers. There were three drawing rooms, a great and little dining room, two galleries and three halls. At least twenty-four of the rooms were for living-in servants and were generally named according to their occupants rather than by their occupations. The exceptions were those of the cook, steward, gardener and laundry maid.

The family's principal apartments (where visiting Royalty would have stayed) were the King's room with a small adjoining room, the King's drawing room and closet, the Lord's dressing room, the Queen's room and Queen's drawing room. A gatehouse chamber and gallery led to the main drawing room and dining rooms. These chambers were luxuriously furnished with expensive fabrics, carpets and furniture of Eastern character.

Amongst the items contained in the King's room was a crimson velvet bed with a gold and silver lace fringe, lined with flowered satin and a set of white feathers. There were four chairs and six stools of the same material and two elbow chairs covered in red damask. The bed and bolster were of down and were covered by three fine blankets, a large Holland quilt and a large Indian quilt. Also itemised was a 36 inch mirror with table and stand and a pair of striped calico curtains and valance, while in the hearth were a pair of brass andirons, some bellows and a brush. Perhaps the most valuable contents of the room were six pieces of fine tapestry "containing" 223 ells, being 5½ ells deep. If one ell equals forty-five inches, then almost certainly the walls of the King's room were completely covered by this tapestry. At the time the inventory was taken the contents of the room were valued at £164. In the King's drawing room with adjoining closet were a further four large pieces of tapestry, a six-leaf screen 8ft. high, two calico window curtains, two sconces (lanterns possibly for candles) — two old pictures, all valued at £60. Similarly the Queen's room contained four fine tapestries embroidered with gold arms and corners. A gold damask bed was lined with a white "pealeing" embroidered in silk with a matching quilt: the feather bed and bolster were covered with three blankets and a calico quilt, while on the floor the velvet carpet was fringed with gold. Also in the room were six elbow chairs, a black table and stand and a 36 inch mirror. there were two white Persian window curtains and a "Parragan" case, which could have been a case for cloaks made of costly Eastern materials. The contents were valued at £12 10s.

Amongst the furniture in the Queen's drawing room were two elbow chairs covered in green "crocodile" with a mixed fringe. Six smaller chairs and a stool were covered likewise. There were also eight large and four small pictures. In the gallery three fine Turkey carpets were to be found, with four other large carpets. The drawing room yet again contained six pieces of fine tapestry, three pictures, steel fire-dogs and andirons. The assessment of over £50 for these few articles must reflect the high value placed on the tapestries in this room.

Furniture in the great dining room comprised fourteen further chairs which may have been covered with wool woven to give an appearance of Turkish carpets, and three stools probably covered in the same material. There were two carpets, six pieces of tapestry and the only clock and case in the inventory. There were many pictures in the family's rooms at Place House, but the main collection was housed in the gallery where there were twenty-five large pictures and twenty-two small ones. These, together with the furniture of five stools, a table and one elbow chair of Irish stitched work, were only valued at £10 12s. However, one painting which was probably a gift to the fourth Earl of Southampton, was contained in the Queen's drawing room and is described as Charles I on horseback. Could this have been painted by Van Dyck? The greater part of this collection is now at Welbeck Abbey, once home of the Dukes of

Portland, who inherited part of the Titchfield estates through the marriage of the first Duke to Lady Elizabeth Noel, eldest surviving daughter of Katherine and Wriothesley Baptist Noel.

The servants' rooms were well furnished and comfortable, and with very few exceptions the beds, pillow and bolsters were of feather. There were ample blankets and quilts for coverings, the latter made of calico, fustian, or holland. There was also plenty of furniture, which consisted of tables, chairs, forms, stools and cupboards, while rooms were made warmer by the addition of curtains, rugs, tapestries and wall hangings, as not all the rooms appear to have had firehearths. At this point it is worth noting that the Noels paid £3 13s. twice a year as tax for the seventy-three firehearths in Place House, two lodges and the schoolhouse. The average estimated value of the contents of the servants' rooms was around £3. An interesting point is that the soft furnishings and carpets in the servants' quarters were predominantly green in colour and in the audit room next to Mr. Newsham's chamber the furniture was of green serge and the curtains a green baize.

In 1699 Mr. Clement Newsham, Steward to the ladies, Elizabeth and Rachel Noel, witnessed the valuation and sale of the goods in Place House to Lord Brook. His position in the household obviously demanded suitable quarters. His chamber had an adjoining closet which was unique for a servant, and the contents of his room valued at over £11 were equally impressive. The hangings, although described as old, were of gilt leather, while the bed-head was covered with embroidered cloth. The bed bolster and pillow were feather and covered by a red stitched quilt. The ceiling of the tester bed was covered with a double valance or canopy. In his closet the hangings were again green material and amongst the furniture was a press for his books.

The servants ate in their own hall which contained tables, forms and a cupboard: while in another hall which also appears to be part of the servants' quarters, twelve shovel board pieces separately valued at £1 10s. could represent their indoor recreation. In the same hall amongst the tables, tapestry and Turkey carpet were twenty-three leather buckets. The working accommodation was the kitchen, pantry, dairy, laundry, wash house, stillhouse, cellars and brewery. The cellars and brewhouse contained amongst other items, fifty-eight hogsheads: one large and one small copper, some sieves, scales, two kneading troughs, two small vats to brine the wheat in, an old mash vat and one tun (=252 wine gallons). There was also a large peale (flat shovel), some tongs and a coal rake. We know from other accounts that sea coal brought from Hill Head was used to heat Place House.

The still house next to the brewhouse contained a large copper still with a worm and tub, another large old still, two presses, and a quantity of copper preserving pans showing that some form of spirit was produced. Claret was certainly cellared on the estate in large quantities and in some earlier account books there are references to the brewing of marsh beer, which incorporated beans in the mash as well as malt.

The dairy, laundry and wash house contained the usual items, but some contents of the kitchen are worthy of note. A lead cistern and a large boiler probably supplied the hot water, and cooking was done on a range. Plates, dishes and basins were generally of pewter which when damaged were weighed and given in part exchange for new. There was a further large quantity of pewter dishes and plates, brass, copper and old tin ware amongst sundry articles valued at over £42 in the "ward robe". Those in the kitchen were separately valued and numbered 205 pewter dishes and plates, 31 pewter basins, 30 pieces of brass and 20 of copper. There were only ten glasses and four mugs suggesting that other drinking vessels came under the classification of earthenware or sundry pewter. The sum total of goods assessed was £771 6s. 2d. These were appraised by Nicholas Patrick who bought them on behalf of Lord Brook.

Katherine Sheffield died on 7th February 1704 and was buried in Westminster Abbey. Her daughter Elizabeth was married the following June just before her fifteenth birthday to Henry Bentinck, first Earl of Portland. Her younger sister Rachel married in 1706, aged 16 to Henry Somerset, second Duke of Beaufort, as his second wife. She died three years later shortly following her nineteenth birthday.

REFERENCE:

Hampshire Record Office, 5M53/1444

Veronica Ward

The Bones in the Wall, West Street.

THE BONES IN THE WALL

One of the many unanswered questions in the history of Titchfield is the origins of the bones in the wall in West Street. In West Street, near the sarsen stones and opposite the buildings of the old National School, is a length of wall at least two hundred years old in which bones have been used as courses between the bricks. These bones have been regarded with some superstitious awe for many years. They are not human bones, however, but knuckle bones of sheep. Their number and the regularity of their sizes suggest that they may have come from a slaughter house or some kind of bone-using workshop. But why the bricklayer took the trouble to insert such an irregular material as bones amongst his bricks is a problem. Was he really so poor that waste bones were cheaper than bricks? Were the bones intended to be ornamental? Or did they serve as a drainage channel for the earth bank against which the wall is built? We may never know. The wall is now (1989) in a poor, crumbling state, and it would be a pity if this intriguing little detail of local history were allowed to disappear.

George Watts

SOME PARISH RECORDS

Among the parish records are Apprenticeship Indentures; the years covered are from 1683 to 1739. Each indenture is for a "poor child" and there are eighty nine of these altogether — fifty eight for boys and thirty one for girls.

Of the boys, fifty one are apprenticed to the "art, mistery or occupation of a Husbandman", usually for a farm or estate of which the owner is sometimes a magistrate, a churchwarden or an overseer. Two boys are each apprenticed to a "mariner" who (1719) possessing the "art of a Mariner which he now useth shall teach and instruct ...the best way and manner that he can see". One boy is bound to a bricklayer; in four indentures the trade to be learned is not mentioned although, as the masters are designated either yeoman or farmers, it is almost certainly husbandry.

Twenty eight of the girls are apprenticed to the "art of a Housewife or Housewiferie" while two more are put to "Husbandry and Household work", and (1704) one master "shall teach and inform or cause to be taught and informed such workes as are fit and necessary for one of her condition to learne". All but six of the children are apprenticed in Titchfield itself. One boy goes to Hound and another to Rowner to learn husbandry. Portsea gets one girl for housewiferie, and also an apprentice to the "Boatswain of his Majesties Ship the Southsea Castle". A Gosport mariner takes a boy for his own trade and the lad's sister for housewiferie, perhaps so that they should not be separated.

In the earliest indentures (1683) a boy is apprenticed until he reaches the age of twenty one years (this is the only indenture in connection with which there was a bond, because of a cash payment to the master, who resided in another parish). With the second (1693) and all the other indentures for boys the finishing age is "Twenty fowar. According to the Statute". For girls the apprenticeship is always until she "shall accomplish her full Age or the day of her Marryage".

At what age were the children apprenticed? In most cases the age is not given, but it is given in eleven as follows:-

Boys	Apprenticed to a Mariner at age of 14 years in 1719
	1733 Apprenticed to Husbandry at age of 7 years
	1735 Apprenticed to Husbandry at age of 10 years
	1736 Apprenticed to Husbandry at age of 9 years
	1737 Apprenticed to Husbandry at age of 10 years
	1737 Apprenticed to Husbandry at age of 11 years
Girls	1733 Apprenticed to housewifery at age of 8 years
	1737 Apprenticed to housewifery at age of 9 years
	1737 Apprenticed to housewifery at age of 10 years
	1737 Apprenticed to housewifery at age of 10 years
	1737 Apprenticed to housewifery at age of 14 years

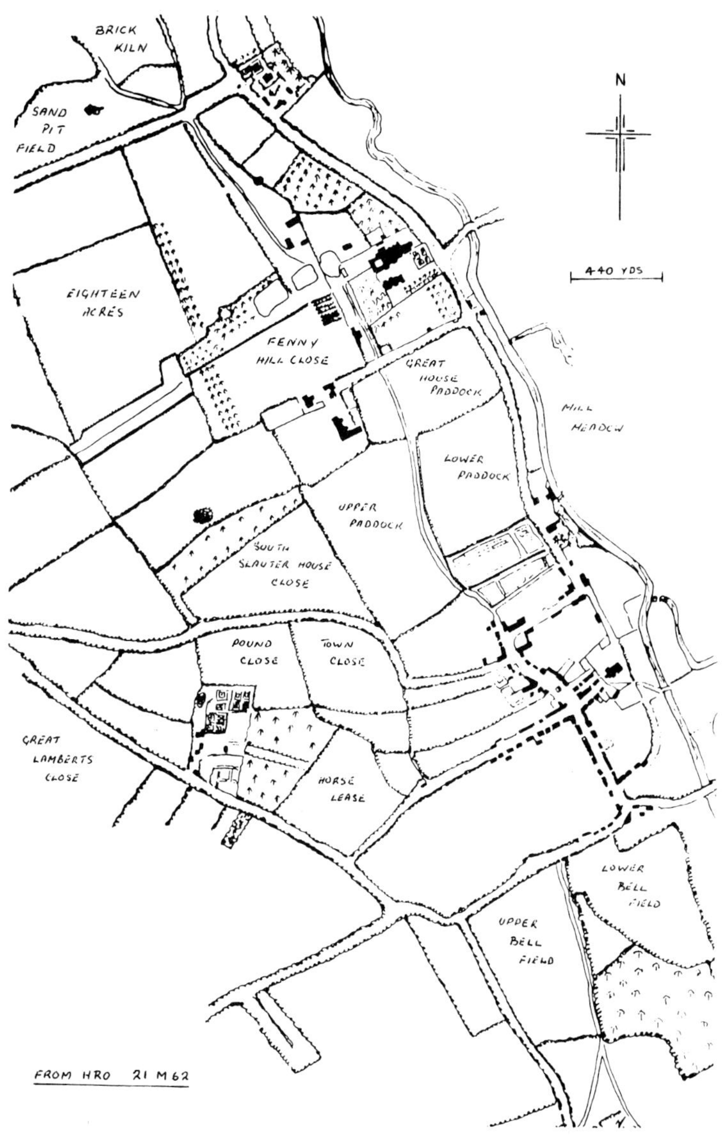

Titchfield in the middle of the Eighteenth Century.

In drawing conclusions from these cases one must bear in mind that they represent only 12½% of the apprentices recorded. Nevertheless they may give some useful pointers. The average starting age of the boys is 9 years and if the boy who goes to sea in the "Southsea Castle" is left out the age is 8 years. For girls the average age is 10 years, and if the last child is omitted it drops to 9 years.

In two cases the children bear the same name as the master to whom they are apprenticed. In 1733 John Buckett is bound to John Buckett, and in 1737 William Tayler is bound to Arthur Tayler. Could these boys have been in some way adopted?

In 1705, Robert White of Crabthorne, Yeoman, takes a boy to learn husbandry and twenty years later takes another. Similarly, in 1712, John Missing, Magistrate, takes a boy for the Posbrook Farm and takes another fifteen years later.

The following is a sample of the form the indentures took:—

"This indenture witnesseth that Charles Binstead, son of Richard Binstead late of ye parish of Titchfield in ye countie of Southt. By ye appointment and agreement of ye Churchwarden and Overseers for ye poor of ye said parish is bound forth apprentice in husbandry to John West of ye parish of Hound in ye said countie, Yeoman, untill he ye said Charles shall attain to ye age of twentie one years. During which terme ye said master his said apprentice shall keepe and allow unto him all necessary food and clothing. And in the end of ye said terme shall and will give unto his said apprentice double apparell meet and convenient for such an apprentice to have and were. In witness whereof to ye one part of these present indentures the said Churchwardens and Overseers have set their hands and seales. To ye other part thereof the said Master hath set his seal Dated in ye Thirtie Ffith yeare of ye raigne of our Soveraigne Lord Charles ye second King over England...

In the presence of	John West
Thomas Houghton	X
Wm. Houghton	his mark"

Other bonds are most interesting and human documents — made for a variety of reasons. There are twelve of them and they extend from 1683 to 1755.

In 1683, Richard Ward, Henry Stevens and Thomas Payne asked permission for Richard Ward of Rumsey "to become an inhabitant of Titchfield" and this is allowed if they sign a bond, which they consent to do.

In 1688, Thomas Lymeburner of Portsmouth is given "Thirty shillings of Lawfull money of England" by "ye churchwardens and overseers for ye poor to take Sarah Lymeburner daughter of Thomas Lymeburner

Snr. late of ye parish of Titchfield aforesaid Apprentice untill the age of twentie one yeares or the day of her marriage and to well and truly save, defend and keep harmless ye said parrish of and from all costs charges and incumbrances whatsoever". He is bound in £20. So Thomas takes his sister off the Titchfield rates for thirty shillings.

In 1693, Richard Holte of Crofton, yeoman, is bound in £60, but he receives rather more than Thomas Lymeburner. He agrees to take "Elinor and Mary Underwood Daughters of John Underwood late of ye parish of Titchfield aforesaid Deceased, to maintain, breed up and keep ye said Elinor and Mary untill the age of Twentie one yeares or dayes of Marriadge". For doing this he receives £24.

On 21st April, 1703, William Cleverley of Hound, yeoman, signs a bond whereby the churchwardens and overseers agree to receive William's daughter and her husband Edward Newman. This however is a temporary affair "till or before 24 June next" to enable Edward to get a lease for five or more acres of land of £10 upwards yearly value in Bursledon. With two months to arrange this William must have been confident, as his bond was for £200!

In 1716, Philip Coats of Melcombe Horsey in Dorset, a labourer, brought a settlement certificate to Titchfield for himself and his family for their "advantage and better support". In 1738, he dies and leaves one child, Elizabeth. Then Henry Coat, Labourer, of Piddlehinton, Dorset, undertakes the responsibility for the maintenance of the girl, but he receives no reward for so doing. Instead, he is bound in £30.

In 1718, John Brock of Titchfield husbandman and Thomas Fox of Hamble sign a bond in £40 that a loan of £20 10s. 0d. shall be repaid "on or upon the Twelfth day of May next ensuing". It seems a large loan and there is no evidence of its purpose.

A most beautifully written bond, perhaps the best looking of all the documents, is that of Charles Freebury, who undertakes to marry Allice Churcher for which he receives "The sum of three Pounds as a Consideration", but he also promises to maintain and keep her daughter Jane Churcher. The bond is for £50 and the date 1726. The historian W.E. Tate suggests that Overseers sometimes paid the father of an illegitimate child to marry the mother, but there is no evidence of this here; Charles lives at Chichester.

In 1727, a glover of Bishop's Waltham signs a bond in £100 because his wife Mary is near the time of childbirth and in Titchfield (and perhaps cannot travel home) so that the Overseers may rest assured that the baby's maintenance will be provided for.

In 1742, Benjamin and Daniel, both blacksmiths of Titchfield are bound in £20 for Benjamin "lately went away from the aforesaid Parish of Titchfield and left his wife Mary a charge upon the same but hath promised and undertaken not to offend in the like manner for the future", not only for the sake of his wife and her chargeability but also "by Reason of the Birth Maintenance Education or bringing up of any child or children she may hereafter have".

In 1755, Elizabeth McLaughlin and two children intrude into the Parish and a James Hicks, blacksmith of Wells in Somerset is bound in £20 that he will indemnify the parish from possible charges.

Paternity bonds, because of prospective or actual paternity of illegitimate children, number 48 and cover the years of 1692 to 1806. The occupation of five of the men are not specified; of the remainder, the variety is shown by the following list:- Gent.(2), Esquire (2), Yeoman (6), Attorney at Law, Breeches Maker, Shoemaker, Miller, Carpenter, Blacksmith, Tallow Chandler (2), Tanner, Fisherman, Husbandman (3), Forgeman, Cordwainer, Fishmonger, Innholder, Labourer (14), making a total of 41. As two men are bound twice, the man's occupation is given in 43 cases.

Until 1735, the first part of the bonds is written in Latin — "Noverint universi.." but later the whole document is translated into English — "Be it known unto all men.."

In 1692, a man is bound in "Viginti libris bone at legalis monetal Angl.." (£20 of good and legal money of England) but in the next bond, in 1710, the term used is "Monete Magn Britannis" (money of Great Britain) — following the Act of Union between England and Scotland in 1707.

In 1710, also, the amount of the bond is increased from £20 to £100, and this is kept for the next five bonds, until 1728. From 1731 to 1757 this sum, for 13 bonds, is either £40 or £50, and after that £100 is the usual amount. Sometimes the alleged father of the child is bound along with another man, such as his own father, a brother, a friend or an employer, while in two cases there are three and in one case four men bound together. In three instances the accused man is not among those bound over. In 1733, a fishmonger is bound in £50 for his son, but in 1717 the accused man's father-in-law is bound in £100, and in 1776, although the man concerned is a yeoman, it is the girl's grandfather, an Esquire, who is bound in £100. Nineteen bonds were made before and twenty eight after the birth of the child. Three of the women concerned are widows.

A yeoman is bound over twice, once in £40 and then in £50, for two children born to the same mother. In the list also appears a Gent. who signs a bond on two occasions in £100. A Justice of the Peace had a "natural Daughter" and it would appear that no action was taken, but when this happened a second time the Churchwardens and Overseers acted and he signed a bond for £400.

Sometimes it is a Churchwarden or an Overseer or even a Magistrate who was tempted and did wrong, but all seemed to have continued in their office, as shown by their signatures on later documents. The bond safeguarded the rates, making provision for the unfortunate child and giving perhaps indirect help to the mother. One gets the impression, however, that the offence is not regarded as heinous.

In 1806, a labourer and his father are bound in £50 and ordered to pay £3 for the confinement, plus also 2s. per week for 22 weeks after the child shall have ceased to be chargeable — and this bond was made before the child was born. There was a financial deterrent to breaking the seventh commandment, for failing to keep the Parish indemnified might mean prison.

In 1732, a child "born in a place extra parochiall" is residing with her mother in Titchfield and so "may become chargeable to the parishoners of the said parish by reason of its residence". The father, a yeoman of Titchfield, and another yeoman are bound together in £40, and the indemnity is to last for the "full term of seven years to be accompted and reckoned from the day of this date" and then "they will still be responsible until the said child shall by some act or acts . . . gain a legal settlement within the sd.psh. of Titchfield or some other parish". This reference to age is interersting and may envisage a possible early apprenticeship.

One case, in 1750, reminds us of the possibility that a man might be compelled to pay maintenance although it was not certain that he was the father of the child. A great deal must have rested on the character and ability of the Justice of the Peace in doubtful cases. The girl, a Singlewoman, "was about five years past or upwards delivered of a Female Bastard Child" and now charged Edward Clewer, of Bishop's Waltham, with paternity. Edward and John Clewer "to prevent any Law Suite or Expenses ....and for no other reason whatever, have agreed" to be bound in £50 to keep the Parish indemnified.

The Intrusion Orders date from 1724 to 1793. All the forms are printed, although out of the five at Titchfield, there are four with different wording to the same effect. In every case it is the parishes into which the intruders had come which were ordered to take them back into their own parish. Three families are to be returned to Titchfield from Alverstoke, Bletchingly and North Stoneham; and two families are to be taken from Titchfield to Alverstoke and Shaftesbury. John Coles, a labourer, with his wife and six children are found to have come into the parish without giving notice in writing as required under the 1662 Act, as amended in 1685. None of them has a certificate and all of them are likely to be chargeable to the rates.

Mr Wolfe's milk cart from Fern Hill Farm.

The Voluntary Examinations cover the years 1756-1779 and in all there are twenty eight of them, including twenty six "Single Women" and two "Spinsters". Twenty three of these sworn statements were taken before the birth of a child and five after. The first paper is in 1756 and the next is in 1767. From then until 1779 there are twenty seven examinations. While provision for the examination might be said to help a girl who had been led astray by a promise of marriage from a man who had no intention of keeping his word, the danger of an uncorroborated accusation could be very real at times.

The occupation of all the accused are given and were as follows:-

Labourers	14	Carpenters	1
Husbandman	1	Wheelwrights	1
Servants to farmers	2	Bricklayers	1
Gardeners	2	Marines	2
Shoemakers	2	Lieutenant in the Navy	1

An illegitimate child gained a settlement in the parish where is was born and the Overseers had a duty to prevent new demands on the Poor Rate. The procedure was to seek a Magistrate's warrant for the apprehension of the alleged father in order to obtain security for indemnifying the parish against any expense from the expected inhabitant. The case selected here contains a short settlement examination complete with a voluntary examination and a magistrate's opinion. It is the only instance of its kind:

"Southampton (to wit) Elizabeth Privett now residing in the parish of Bursledon in the said county Spinster on her examination on oath saith that she was born in the Parish of Durley in the said county and is about twenty four years of age as she believes, that at Michaelmas now upwards of four years past she hired herself to the wife of Mr John Whittam to serve her for one year at the wages three guineas and a half, that she served her said mistress during the year agreed from Michaelmas then next for one year in the parish of Titchfield and received her wages agreed for and hath not since done any Act to gain a settlement to her knowledge".

Sworn at Fareham 4th day of October 1772.

"Southampton. Elizabeth Privett now residing in the Parish of Titchfield in the County of Southampton Single Woman on her Voluntary Examination on Oath saith that she is with child and that James Gorey now residing in the Parish of Botley in the said county, labourer, is the father of the child or children and that the said child or children when born is or are likely to become chargeable to the said

parish of Titchfield and that she is more than seven months gone with child".
Sworn at Titchfield 26th day of November 1772.

27th Nov. 1772. James Gorey appears. Elizabth Privett resworn "and he don't deny the fact". He is invited to marry the girl, find security or be committed. Thomas Gorey his brother appears but will not be bound nor can he find any security for the parish or for sufficient Sureties for his appearance at the next General Quarter Sessions.

"There appears a clear Settlement gained by Elizabeth Privett in the Parish of Titchfield but she has since lived a year and a half under a general hiring with her Brother the latter part of which was in the Parish of Hound and as that was more than forty days I am inclined to think her settlement is now in the Parish of Hound.

If the man marries her as he is now in custody under a warrant granted by Mr. Ives on the woman to Voluntary Information of his getting her with child I think after the ceremony he may be carried before the Justice to be Discharged from that warrant and if another Justice of the Peace should then be with Mr. Ives he may then be examined as to his Parish and an order of Removal made at once.

S. Missing, Catisfield 27th November 1772".

REFERENCE:

The original documents are in the Hampshire Record Office, 37M73A, PO1-PO73

W.J. Shaw

THE MISSING FAMILY

In the ancient Crofton Church is a fine monument to Thomas Missing. The inscription reads:

Underneath are deposited
the Remains of
Thomas Missing
Late of Stubington in the County of Southampton Esqre
Who was born the 10th day of February 1675. And died the 6th day of July 1733
A Gentleman much regretted at his Death
Because much beloved in his Life.
As a Private Man
He was assiduous in the Offices of Humanity:
In those of Justice as a Magistrate
In those of Publick Spirit as a Senator:
An honourable Employment acquired by his Merits
He Possessed with Esteem,
Because he discharged it with Integrity.
Nor was a large Fortune
Acquired by his honest Abilities
Attended with Envy,
Since it was acquired without Baseness or Blemish
And employed in acts of Benevolence.
To the honest and diligent he was a sure Patron and Friend
To the Idle and Vitious Severe without Cruelty;
A warm Champion for Publick Liberty,
And for the pure Religion of Peace and Truth;
An Adversary to all Bigotry and Pious Folly
As dishonouring the great Creator and pernicious to ye Creation.
Piety towards God he knew
To be ever accompanied with tenderness towards Men
Whilst Imposture delighted in Rage and Terrors
Such was the Character such the Sentiments and Religion
of Mr. Missing, Dearest to those who knew him most,
And like him loved Virtue best.
Reader
Applaud and Imitate

This Thomas was an agent to the Navy at Gosport and Portsmouth, one of whose concerns was the victualling of Gibraltar after its acquisition by Britain. Two later Thomas Missings were Recorders of Romsey. A John Missing, perhaps uncle of the first Thomas, was churchwarden of Crofton in 1674 and a parish overseer in 1681. Another

THE SOUTH EAST VIEW OF

Tychfield Abby, was founded by Peter de Rupibus Bishop
of K. H. 6th with Margaret of Anjou was here solemniz'd. It
Male, it came by Marriage of his Daughter, to Edward 1st Ear
present Proprietors are, his Grace ye Duke of Beaufort & her Gra

Place House 1733.

ELD ABBY, IN HAMPSHIRE.

y.e 16.th of K.H.3.rd for Premonstratension Canons. The Marriage
riothesly Earl of Southampton; but he dying without Issue
h: and for want of Issue Male again to two Daughters. The
e Portland. An. Val. { £ 249 .. 16 .. } Dug. ; { 280 .. 19 .. } Speed.

S. & N. Buck delin. et Sculp.t 1733.

John was a magistrate in 1712 and 1727; and it was probably his son, yet another John, who wrote the long poem about Titchfield which was published in 1749. The Missings were very active in the affairs of the ancient parish throughout the eighteenth century, living at various times at Crofton, Stubbington, Catisfield, Hillhead and Posbrook. S. Missing, another magistrate, was living in Catisfield in 1772. Richard Missing was described as a barrister in the 1830 Directory, and was chairman of the meeting held to revive the village market in 1832. Richard may have been the last of the Titchfield Missings, but the family had played an important part in the district for over 150 years, and their story deserves further research.

Trevor Cox

The Missing Memorial in Crofton Church.

PLACE HOUSE IN 1737

The plans of the ground and first floors of Place House or Titchfield House as drawn by John Achard in 1737 are of great interest. 200 years had elapsed between the dissolution of the monastery and this survey. There must have been many alterations and additions since 1538 but these were probably only of a minor character. The plan printed here has been simplified and the spelling modernised from the original in the Hampshire Record Office.

What is of particular interest is the central feature — the hall. This and the adjoining rooms follow the general pattern of medieval buildings. The entrance is to one end of the hall with a through passage separating it by a screen in which are two openings or doorways. Over this passage is the minstrels' gallery. To the left of the passageway or entrance is the buttery or pantry with the kitchen adjoining. At the other end of the hall is the solar with an oriel window. What is unusual is that the hall floor is some feet above ground level — the survey states that there are "20 steps, each one a foot broad" to the entrance. If we assume each step to have a 5in. rise then the level of the hall floor would be 8ft 4ins above ground level. This is confirmed by the fact that the beer and wine cellars have windows or openings to the kitchen court. The cellars would be partly below ground and it is noted that they are arched, which would mean a barrel type vault or, I think, quadri-partite vaulting. In view of this the hall floor is more likely to be stone paved or laid with tiles. There are also indications of a large fireplace in the north wall of the hall.

There is another aspect to be noted — the hall has lost some of its medieval importance. Then the hall was the centre of all activities: eating, socialising and even sleeping, and in the early days there would have been a central fire with the smoke escaping through the roof. Here at Titchfield we have a drawing room, a large and small dining room, together with a long gallery at first floor level. In Elizabethan times there was more contact with the continent and information was brought back, particularly from Italy of the noble classical palaces. These palaces were usually built around a square and the principal rooms were on the first floor (Piano nobile), usually approached by an ornate staircase. Here at Titchfield the layout has not quite reached the classical style — there is no grand staircase, but we do have the principal rooms at first floor level. One would say that the layout is in a transitional stage. To quote from Banister Fletcher's A History of Architecture. "The reign of Elizabeth (1558-1603) witnessed the establishment of the Renaissance style in England". Elizabethan architecture which followed the Tudor was a transitional style, with Gothic features.

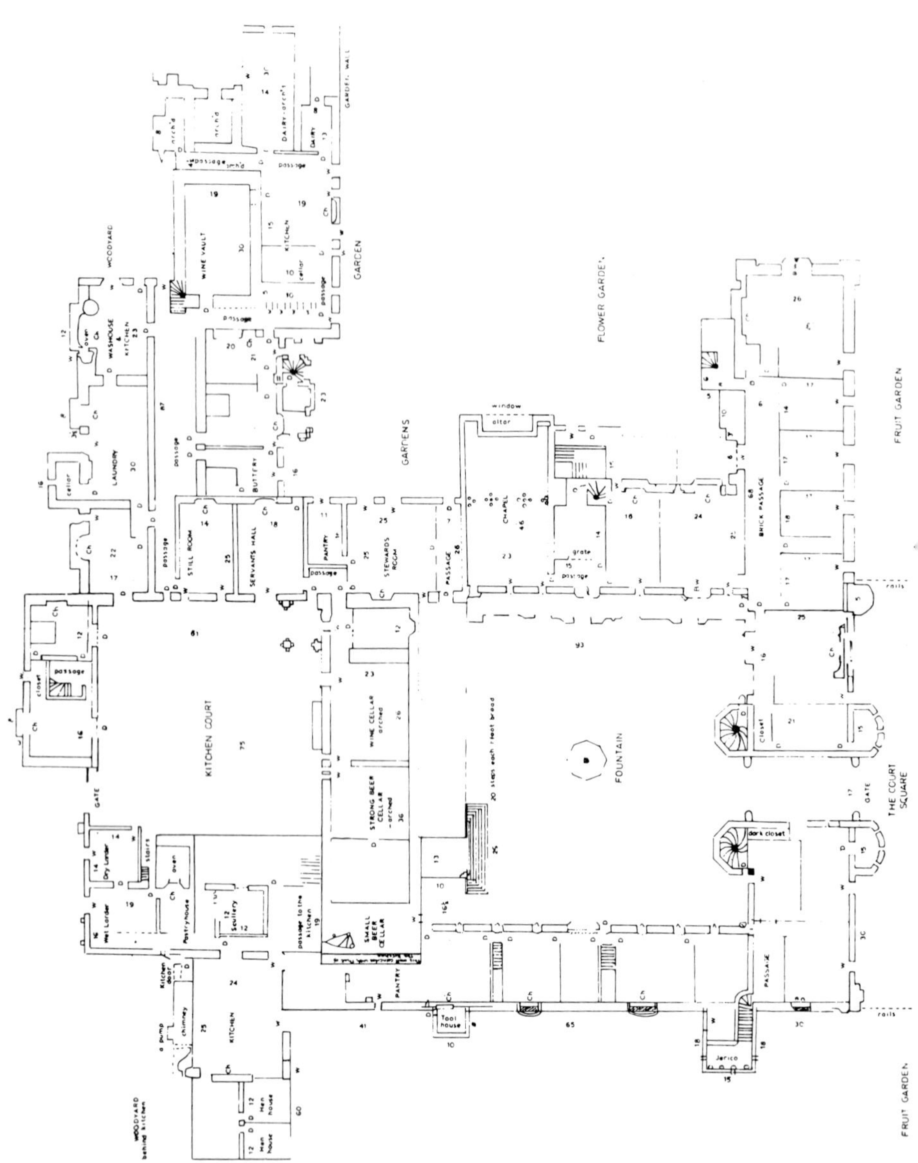

John Achard's plan of Place House is remarkably consistent with the surviving engravings of the south-east and the north-west aspects of the House. The north-west view however needs some explanation. The view shown looking into the kitchen court does not quite fit with the plan. The view seems to be somewhat earlier in date because the wet and dry larders are not shown (presumably because they were not then there) and as a

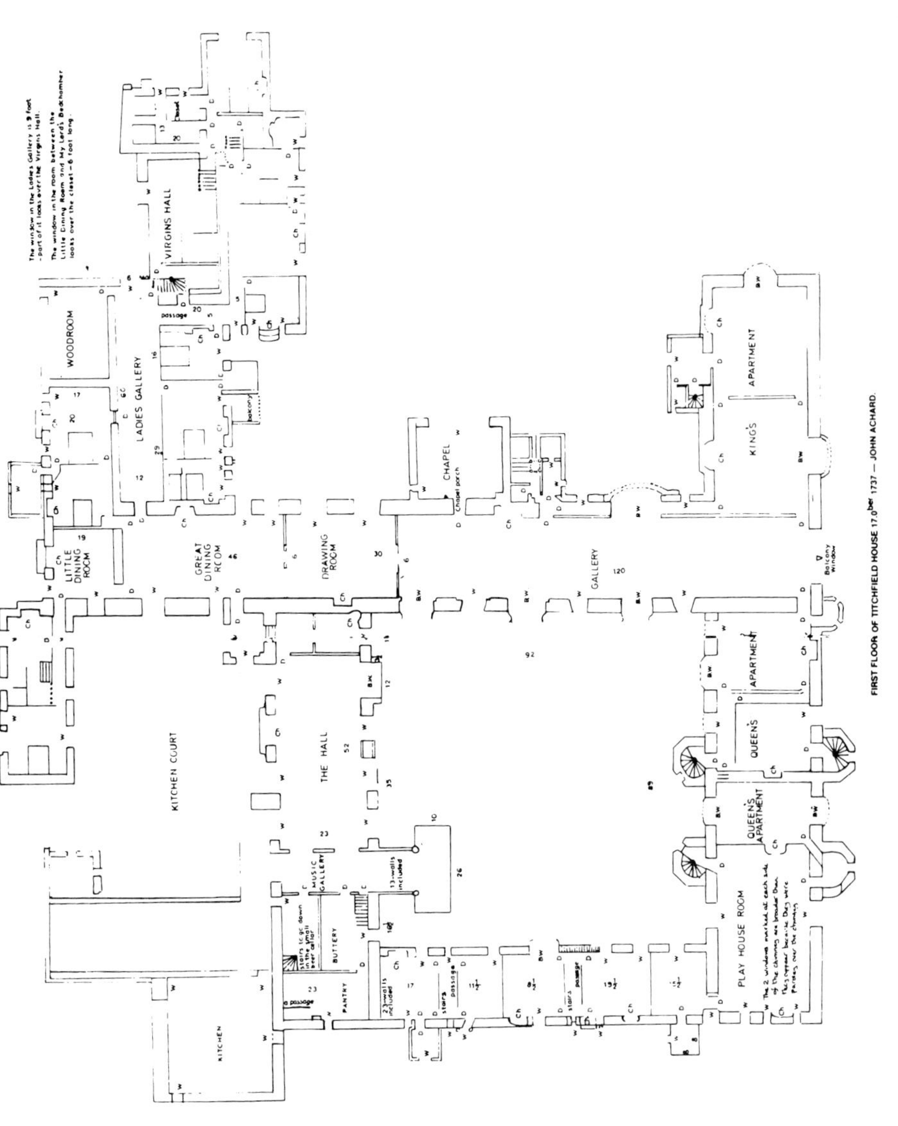

result the chimney of the pastryhouse oven appears on the outer wall of the building. Parts of the building shown on the left of the picture (including the laundry, a washhouse and a kitchen) were probably incorporated later into the house which still (1989) stands immediately to the north of Place House.

The kitchen 25ft×24ft is situated close to the buttery and pantry and was probably two stories in height. There is a wide fireplace opening (about 16ft wide) with four windows high up in the walls. Adjoining the kitchen are the usual ancillaries, scullery, pastry house (with oven), dry larder, wet larder, and all backing on to the woodyard. What is not clear is how, or more particularly by what route hot food from the kitchen was taken to the great dining room, a distance of some 30 yards.

The hall forms the north side of a quadrangle — Fountain Court. The entrance is on the south side. This entrance is stated to be 17ft wide between walls and some 25ft long, with apparently strong wooden gates at either end. On each side of the gateway are flanking towers — part octagonal — as now existing. On either side of the main entrance — the south front — are rooms on the ground floor, the purpose of which is not indicated. There are two rooms to the left (west) but the right (east) has a projection to the east containing further rooms, seven in number. Five of these rooms have a passage or corridor to provide access. This fact is mentioned because elsewhere access is only provided from room to room. Passageways or corridors were not always provided in this period as at Hampton Court for instance.

The first floor (southern front) has some very important rooms. They are from west to east, playhouse room (probably a small theatre) approx. 41ft ×24ft, then three rooms interconnecting and named 'Queen's Appartments', 24ft×16ft, 20ft×16ft and 24ft×20ft approximately. Immediately next, the end of the long gallery terminates at the south front wall with a balcony window. Again continuing eastwards to the south front are the 'King's Appartments' consisting of two rooms 29ft×24ft and 28ft×24ft approximately, the end room having a balcony window facing east.

The ground floor (west front) comprises five rooms — all interconnecting plus two staircases leading to the first floor. At the southern end of the block is a projecting room marked "jerico", meaning toilets. Presumably the common name for chamber pot — jerry — is derived from Jericho. This room provides a conundrum: there is a staircase shown as the approach thereto — if ground floor, the staircase would appear to connect at the first floor with the playhouse room, but no stairs are shown at this point at the first floor. Could the jericho be partly below ground? It could serve the several rooms here, but what about lighting and ventilation?

The ground floor (east front) consists of three fairly large rooms interconnected as is also a chapel 46ft long × 23ft wide, the axis being west to east. Next to the chapel is a passage leading from Fountain Court to the gardens. Next again further north is the steward's room, 25ft×25ft with a chimney which shows the importance of his office. Proceeding northwards is the pantry, servants' hall, still room, etc., and then eastwards, the laundry, washhouse, buttery, kitchen and minor rooms.

The first floor (east side) provides the more important rooms — the long gallery, approximately 120ft×21ft, the end wall of which terminates in the external wall to the south front (giving access on either side to the King's and Queen's apartments). There is a balcony window at the southern end and also a large bay window facing east. There is a feature shown here which is not properly understood. On the survey, a door is shown directly over the chapel with the note "chapel porch". Was it possible that one could open the door and stand on a small balcony, a kind of gallery in the chapel itself and view the high altar and even watch the service below? There is also a large fireplace situated in the east wall. Passing through from the gallery northwards, one enters the drawing room, approximately 46ft×21ft, and thence northwards is the little dining room 19ft×18ft. Each of these have fireplaces. Situated on the first floor over the cluster of rooms to the north east are several bedrooms and also the ladies' hall and virgin's hall (presumably for young women).

There are still a lot of imponderables and obvious errors in the plan, for instance the route of service to the great dining room; certain thicknesses are dubious — the walls on the first floor east block are about twice the thickness of those on the ground floor. In addition to what is shown there must have been stabling, coach and cart sheds, cattle sheds, piggeries and other outbuildings. However this survey does provide some very useful knowledge of the layout of Place House. It can be compared with the rooms described in the list of furnishings in 1699, and with the only view we have of the house from the north before its partial demolition by the Delmés.

REFERENCE:

Hampshire Record Office, 5M53/55.

Arthur Tamkin

EDWARD IVES

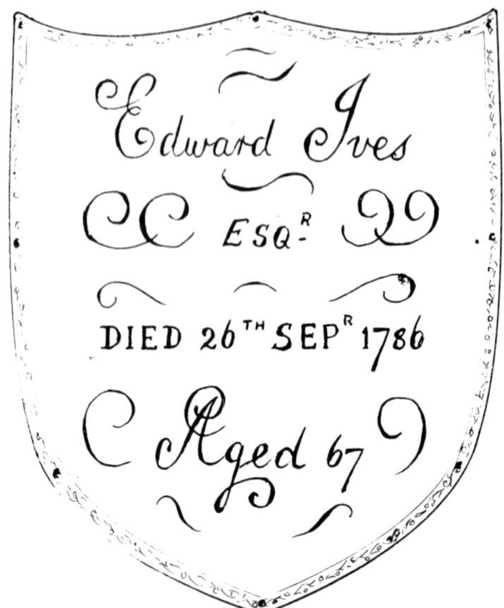
Edward Ives
ESQ^R
DIED 26TH SEP^R 1786
Aged 67

Coffin Plate.

In the chancel of Titchfield Church are monuments to Edward Ives and his son Edward Otto Ives. Edward Ives was born at Lymington on 9th February 1719, and became a naval surgeon. He served on the "Namur" in the Mediterranean from 1744-1746, and then for a while was employed by the Commissioners for the sick and wounded. From 1753-1757 he served on the "Kent" under Vice-Admiral Watson, and sailed to India. He remained there until his resignation in 1757, and then returned to England overland, arriving 1759. He spent his last years at Titchfield, dividing his time apparently between literature and farming, and died at Bath on 25th September, 1786. In about 1751 he had married Ann daughter of Richard Roy of Titchfield; they had several children, of whom one, Edward Otto, became prominent in the service of the East India Company and died in Titchfield.

In 1773 Edward Ives published an account of his travels: "A voyage from England to India in the year MDCCLIV ... also a journey from Persia to England by an unusual route". In this book he shows an awareness of the important work of Dr. James Lind of Haslar Hospital on scurvy, the disease now known to be caused by Vitamin C deficiency, but which at that time was little understood and which often devastated ships' crews on long voyages. Ives reports having largely avoided the problem on his ship by giving orange or lemon juice daily to the crew in accordance with Lind's recommendations, and that the crews of the other ships, on which this treatment was not available, were very badly affected.

Conclusive proof of the value of citrus fruit as an anti-scorbutic came only with the isolation of Vitamin C in the early 1930s. However, the circumstantial evidence was too good to be sensibly ignored, and it is a sad commentary on human fallibility (if no worse) that scurvy and its remedy long continued to be a matter of some controversy, and that many voyages and expeditions, including Captain Scott's South Polar Expedition suffered unnecessarily as a result. Edward Ives was a pioneer.

Keith Hayward

Footnote — a face to face encounter with Edward Ives.
In the course of digging foundations for the new Chapter Rooms in July 1989 a brick vault was discovered, sited just inside the south-west corner of the old pre-1866 south aisle of the church. The vault contained a substantial lead coffin, now largely decayed. The coffin plate was recovered and reads "Edward Ives Esq.; died 26 Sept 1786; Aged 67". There was a small hole in the top of the lead coffin, which enabled a brief examination of the skeleton to be made with the aid of a torch. While no proper pathological examination was possible, we can safely say that Edward Ives suffered from very bad teeth!

Michael Hare

CRIME AND PUNISHMENT 1780-1850

The era of the stage-coaches, racing from town to town with horns sounding and pulling up at inns like the Bugle and the Coach and Horses for convivial refreshment, was to become idealised in the late nineteenth century in an image of the Good Old Days. But that period had a much darker side, of poverty, violence, crime and harsh punishment, a side of life which in Titchfield can be illustrated from the Calendar of Prisoners in Winchester Gaol which was kept for the use of the justices in Quarter Sessions.

First, there were severe sentences. On Boxing Day 1788, for instance, John Bulford, aged 33, was committed to the Gosport Bridewell and thence to the Winchester Bridewell, for stealing six fowls, the property of the Reverend Henry Taylor of Titchfield. A few days later, at the January Quarter Sessions, Bulford was sentenced to seven years' transportation. In January 1825 William Thomas, aged 15, stole a sixpenny piece and 2½d., the property of Sarah Franklin, widow, of Titchfield, and was sentenced to seven years' transportation. And in 1844 William Olding, aged 26, stole a smock frock and a whip, the property of Charles Gray, and a piece of rope called a cart-line, the property of Thomas Marshall: he got 14 years' transportation.

Then there was whipping. You could be publicly whipped as part of your sentence. For example, in 1833 James Monday, aged 24, stole a wooden two-quart bottle from James Turner. He was given three months' hard labour and twice whipped. But you could also be privately whipped if you were caught in the act, the private whipping being counted as part of the sentence, and not rendering the person doing the whipping liable to prosecution for assault. Also in 1833, Joseph Gillett, aged 18, stole six window-curtains, a razor and its case from Charles Muspratt: he got twelve month's hard labour, one month of it to be in solitary confinement, and was twice privately whipped.

Some of the offences seem pathetically trivial and some the simple outcome of poverty and hunger. In 1806, for instance, Sarah Bowden aged 21, stole a muslin cap from Mary Amor, and was given three months' imprisonment. In 1830 Rebecca Linney, aged 17, stole two silk handkerchiefs from the shop of Joseph Hookey, and got twelve months' hard labour. And in 1842 James Morley, aged 60, who could neither read nor write, stole a leg of pork from William Ford, for which he got a month's hard labour.

Crime took many forms. In 1818 William Morgan, aged 28, was committed as a vagrant wandering abroad and begging. When refused poor relief by Richard Nicholson he "conducted himself in a very

Titchfield in the middle of the Nineteenth Century.

disorderly manner and used the most opprobrious language". There was family violence. In 1823 George Penny, aged 28, assaulted his own mother and then John Churcher, constable of Titchfield, when he tried to intervene. There was sexual violence. In 1824, for example, Henry Winter, aged 21, violently assaulted Elizabeth Buckett with intent there and then to commit a rape on the said Elizabeth. It was possible to be imprisoned for being the parent of a bastard child, whether as the father or the mother. In 1788 John Boxall, aged 24, was charged by Patience Case for bastardy: and in 1818 Harriet Edney, aged 34, was charged with being a lewd woman and having a male bastard child chargeable on the parish.

There were criminal gangs and criminal families. In 1827, for instance, Richard Cousins, David Burgess and James Lock were accused of entering the property of Robert Hewitt at night with intent to kill game, Lock being armed with a gun. They were acquitted on this occasion, apparently because they had got out of the copse before they were caught. In 1830 another Richard Cousins, aged 67, perhaps the father of the first, was acquitted of stealing a copper. But the Cousins family chanced their arms too often. When, in the summer of 1832 George Cousins, aged 23 (a brother?) entered the dwelling-house in Titchfield of James Butcher and stole a man's blue coat, a child's petticoat, a child's frock, two half-crowns and three shillings, he got the punitive sentence of 14 years' transportation. And when Richard, now aged 35, reappeared in the following year, for stealing three trusses of clover hay, the property of the same Robert Hewitt whose game he had pursued, he got seven years' transportation. As to James Lock, the one carrying the gun in Hewitt's copse, it was his wife Martha Ann who three years later stole a pair of pattens, a piece of French buckram, a crepe handkerchief and three umbrellas from Joseph Hookey's shop and a piece of printed cotton from James Turner, for which she got twelve months' hard labour. Years later, in 1841, Andrew Lock (son of James and Martha Ann?) got three months' gaol for stealing a beaver hat; Andrew was also with a gang which stole property from Thomas Monday in 1845; and with the gang which attempted the burglary of Fareham Workhouse in 1847, as a result of which yet another Lock (Arthur) was transported.

It was in 1837 that Charles Dickens imagined Mr Pickwick and Sam Weller on the outside of a stage-coach cheerfully arriving at the Angel Inn in Bury St Edmunds: but only a year later he was to create the darker picture of Oliver Twist in the company of Bill Sykes and the Artful Dodger. The Hampshire gaol records show us that this other side of nineteenth century society was not just fiction: it was part of the background to people's lives in quite ordinary communities like Titchfield.

REFERENCE:

Calendars of Prisoners: index volumes (Hampshire Record Office) Q7

George Watts

HUBBARDS MILL AND ITS TENANTS

Hubbard's Mill, almost certainly the Crofton Mill mentioned in Domesday Book, stood on the east bank of the Meon about a mile below Titchfield village. In the early eighteenth century its tenants were the Fryer family. Ann daughter of Henry and Mary Fryer of Hubbards Mill was baptised in 1700. Thomas Fryer of Hubbards Mill married Elizabeth Marsh in 1714, and they had five children between 1715 and 1723 — Mary, John, Ann, Sarah and Robert. When Thomas Fryer himself died in 1723, he was described as of Hubbard Mills. There were also Fryers in Catisfield and later in Titchfield village, in Fareham and on the Isle of Wight.

In the nineteenth century, John Muchatt, described as a labourer, appears as the tenant of Hubbards Mill, with children Louise, Elizabeth and Henry baptised between 1856 and 1871. The buildings on the site, shown on eighteenth and nineteenth century maps, seem by that date to have been occupied only as a cottage. The Jeffries family were living at the mill in the 1920s. The buildings, which presumably had no mains services, seem to have become derelict in the 1930s.

Amongst the rubbish on the site in the early 1980s, however were a number of shaped oak beams which looked as though they had been parts of machinery. By the late 1980s the site had been cleared and levelled.

F.A. Fryer

TITCHFIELD 1809-1845

We are told from a Trade Directory of 1830 that the mouth of the River Alre (evidently an error for the Meon) formed a good roadstead for small vessels which provided an important trade for the town. In 1832 a meeting was held to consider the revival of the market, and Richard Missing was elected Chairman. At the first meeting the principal inhabitants of the town were present including Robert and James Hewitt, George Gough, and Charles Bungay. By the end of the first year 5,600 sheep had been sold, as well as oxen, oats, wheat and barley. We are told that the market was held on Saturday, a pleasure fair on the 14th May and a hiring fair on the 25th September. At the hiring fair labourers among them young boys and girls offered themselves to local farmers who employed them at an agreed wage for the coming six months or twelve months.

From the 1821 Census the population of Fareham is given as 3,677 and that of Titchfield 3,527, but the figures are for the parishes and Titchfield at that time covered 16,000 acres and included Sarisbury, Warsash, Stubbington, Hook and many small hamlets. Agriculture was the most important industry and, as we might expect, there were many horses: ten at Titchfield Park Farm, nine at Segensworth, eight at Great Abshot and the usual number of carts, wagons, dung carts, "rave carts", as well as some machinery: winnowing tackle and thrashing machines. Cows, sheep and rams are mentioned, and peas, wheat and oats are grown. At one farm cheese was made, pork was salted and beer was brewed. A rent of £88 a year was paid at Great Abshot.

Of the important people in the parish we hear of H.P. Delmé of Cams Hall and of his mother who in 1810 distributed two oxen, bread and money to the poor at Christmas. In 1813 the heir, John Delmé, came of age and gave a "sumptuous and plentifully supplied entertainment" on a field opposite Place House. The cloth was laid for 170 and venison, fish, poultry, viands, tarts and rich dessert "spread the festive board". John died in 1815 which "cast a gloom throughout the circle of rank and opulence in the County". In 1830 Miss Delmé of St. Margarets Castel (sic) laid the foundation of the National School in West Street. The mistress was paid £32 a year. During these years Lady Harriet Dickson lived in Mill Street, James Hewett at Posbrook, Robert Hewett at Brownwich, John Hornby at Hook House, Lord Henry Paulet at West Hill, the Rev. William Thresher at the Vicarage; Hollam House was occupied by James Anderson.

Nineteenth Century view of the Abbey by Snape.

When Edward Otto Ives died in 1809 his house is described as having stabling for six horses, a brewhouse, a laundry, a granary, and a piggery, and among the furniture are mentioned mahogany four-poster beds with chintz, fine dimity (a cotton fabric) and other hangings "tastefully fitted up in the first style", a drawing room suite of sixteen japanned elbow chairs, Turkey, Wilton and Kidderminster carpets, two pairs of new globes: a pair of "very curious" ivory urns elaborately carved and mounted with gold and ormolu, a mahogany "pembroke", card and pier tables; chiffoniers, fine screens, superb cut-glass chandeliers, silver mounted knives and forks, dessert sets of Derby, Worcester and Salopian porcelain beautifully painted and gilded, a dinner service of English Nankeen of 400 pieces. William Chase lived in a house in Bellfield with four bedrooms and a drawing room "richly corniced". One house is described as having an excellent water closet (no doubt unusual at that time). A property in East Street is let for £16 a year and one in West Street for £10.

Of industrial activity we hear of a saltworks at Warsash being sold, and in Titchfield we hear of Mr. Jesse Mitchell who owns a manufactory for army accoutrements as well as a house "in the most public part of the town" which has a brewhouse, cowhouse and piggery. John Hobbs is a tallow chandler and soap boiler and J. Suatt is a hair cutter, perfumer and peruke maker. Ladies' ostrich feathers are cleaned, attired or mounted in court or ball plumes. J. Leaton sells linen, wool drapery, silk mercery, hosiery, haberdashery, lace and gloves. Amoore and Sons, brewers and spirit merchants of East Street are managed by Alfred and Charles Amoore (there is a memorial to Charles Amoore in the churchyard). In the Directory for 1830 there are seventy-six trade entries including: seven bakers, six blacksmiths, six boot and shoe makers, an auctioneer, a barrister (Mr. R. Missing); a cooper, a stone and marble mason, a straw hat maker, a tallow chandler, a wheelwright and a stay maker.

In the High Street and the Square there are twenty-one people carrying out a trade of some kind. Mr Gough was the auctioneer, Elizabeth Gough was a grocer, tea dealer, milliner and dressmaker. W. Franklin was a butcher and tallow chandler. E. Monday was a carpenter, joiner, builder, surveyor and Hants., Sussex and Dorset fire office agent; T. Monday was a tanner; J. Turner a cooper, J. Grove a manufacturer of coarse earthenware, J. Suatt was the hairdresser and toy dealer, Harriet Tapper at the Bugle operated a posting house and excise office: J. Jennings was the publican at the Queen's Head, J. Hookey and R.W. Knight were linen and wool drapers, W. Green was a saddler and harness maker, T. Foot a shopkeeper and dealer in sundries, Deborah

Pratt and S. Sabine shopkeepers and bakers. T. Blatherwick and T.A. Ricketts were surgeons. There were thirteen people in East Street operating various trades: eighteen in South Street including a staymaker and three blacksmiths: eight in West Street and two in Church Street. The impression is that most people's needs could be provided in the village. The Post Office was in the High Street. Letters arrived by foot post at 9 a.m. from Fareham and were despatched at 5 p.m.

There was one coach to Bristol and Bath daily, four to Portsmouth and three to Southampton. They each had names: the "Royal Mail" went to Bristol and Bath, the "Sovereign" went from Winchester to Portsmouth and the "York House" from Portsmouth to Southampton. The formation of the Titchfield and Cosham Turnpike Trust in 1810 must have improved the roads and hence made travel easier. In that year Admiral Thompson who lived at Bridge House sued the Turnpike Commissioners because they were going to put the road through a meadow attached to his house "which was a place of pleasing retirement (he was 91) suited to his age and feelings". He was given £500 and then obtained a licence and re-named the house The Titchfield Tavern. Three years later it was sold as an ordinary house.

The inns were used for entertainment and the meeting of societies. The play "She Stoops to Conquer" was performed at the Coach and Horses, and a society met in 1811 to commemorate the Battle of Trafalgar. Friendly Societies met with bands in the village in 1829, heard a sermon in the church and then took part in "handsome dinners" in the various inns. The day, we are told, was spent in convivial and social order. A melon and gooseberry show was held at the Queen's Head. The Coach and Horses had seven bedrooms and a club room 45ft long. It had a neat fly doing good business (a fly was a one-horse covered carriage). Several private schools are mentioned.

In 1836 the Poor House in Mill Street was closed and the contents sold which included fifty-one low bedsteads, an 80 gallon copper, a stone salt mill and a man gin (trap) — (man traps were used at that time to discourage poachers). We have the usual crop of local villains. William Ball, for stealing two sheep, was sentenced to death. Four young men were fined 6s. for playing pitch and toss during the hours of divine service and two who could not pay were put in the stocks for three hours. One man announces that anyone harbouring his wife, Menander Rood Compton, or any of her wearing apparel will be prosecuted.

REFERENCES:

Pigots Directory and the files of the *Hampshire Telegraph*

Richard Wade

GENERAL E.C.A. GORDON

For some twenty years General Gordon of St. Margarets was one of the best known inhabitants of Titchfield, Edward Charles Acheson Gordon was born on 21st May 1827. He entered the Royal Engineers as a Second Lieutenant on 10th December 1845, and was promoted to First Lieutenant the following spring. He served in the Eastern Campaign from 1854 until its close, and was awarded the Turkish Medal and the Order of the Medjidieh. He was then appointed Commissioner on behalf of the British Army for the settlement of accounts with the Turkish Government for the Crimean War. Later he served under the Turkish Government first as inspector of Prisons, then for eight years as a member of their Board of Public Works. In 1865 he was placed in charge of the British Military Cemeteries and government buildings on the Bosphorus, and from 1871-1876 was Assistant Director of Works at the War Office.

By now a Colonel, he was appointed in 1880 a member of the Council of the Bermudas, where he was acting Governor for two short periods in 1880 and 1881, and Administrator in 1882. From August 1882 until he retired as a Major-General in 1885 he was Commandant of the School of Military Engineering at Chatham.

He spent his retirement years at Titchfield, where he was Churchwarden for 19 years, and died on 30th August 1909. He was an active member of the Parish Council. A stained glass window in the South Chapel of Titchfield Church was dedicated to his memory in November 1910. His widow Augusta died 16th January 1919 and there is a monument to them both in the Churchyard.

Keith Hayward

CHANGING TIMES

The second half of the 19th Century saw many changes in the old village, among them the final collapse of the attempt to keep the ancient market in existence; the replacement of the elected village constable by a uniformed officer; and the departure of the lords of the manor, the Delmés, from Cams Hall at Fareham. The *Hampshire Telegraph* often recorded changes like these with graphic detail. The entry for the revival of the market in particular provides an interesting list of the business men of the district in 1850.

9th March 1850. Establishment of Titchfield market. We, the undersigned, being the owners and occupiers of land in the parish of Titchfield, do hereby resolve that it is desirable to establish a market for corn and cattle in the town of Titchfield on every alternate Monday throughout the year and that we will support the same by sending a supply of stock, etc. and soliciting the butchers, dealers and others who so readily gave their attendance at the first market held on Monday 4th inst. to continue the same. The next market will be held on Monday 18th inst.

Charles Brett
William Hornby
Arthur Hornby
William Greene
Richard Wooldridge
T.M. Wilkinson
Robert Hewett
William Whettam
Charles Amoore
Richard Binstead, Jun.
John C. Hoad
William Pink
William Hoar
John Wise
Charles Stares
Robert Collins
William Foster
George Coombe
James Anderson
Raudon Hunter
Henry Waters
George Bell
D. Bartholemew
Thomas Monday
John Read
James Gray
George Gray
Spencer Smith
John J. Ekess
Charles Stares
James Colson
Richard Smith
James Burton
Richard Hewett
Robert R. Brock
Thomas Marshall
Stephen Purkis
James Bungey
Stares & Amoore
Joseph Arundel

29th May, 1886. Thorne, a negro, was charged with being disorderly while intoxicated at Titchfield. The prisoner had gathered a mob round him and was using disgusting language when P.C. Samways ordered him to leave and as he obstinately refused to walk he was conveyed in a wheelbarrow to the Police Station at Fareham.

Meet of Otter Hounds in the Square.

12th May, 1894. Mr Robert Delmé left £1000 to the Vicar and Churchwardens the income to be distributed among the poor. He left the portrait of his grandmother, Lady Betty Delmé by Sir Joshua Reynolds, to his nephew Emilius Charles Delmé Radcliffe (now in a gallery in Washington D.C).

26th May, 1894. Sale of Cams Hall, an estate of 600 acres with a park of 130 acres. The mansion is fitted throughout with electric light and a complete system of modern fire appliances, warmed throughout with hot water pipes, noble dining and drawing room of noble proportions elliptic in shape and effectively decorated: smaller drawing room opening into a fine conservatory sixty feet long, also fitted with electric light, fountains, etc. Two other reception rooms, billiard room, 20 principal, secondary and servants' bedchambers, dressing and bathrooms.

Richard Wade

The High Street c., 1910.

SIR STEPHEN GLYNNE'S DESCRIPTION OF TITCHFIELD CHURCH

Sir Stephen Richard Glynne was born in 1807 and lived until his death in 1874 at Hawarden Castle in Flintshire (now Clwyd). He enjoyed a minor career in public life, serving as Liberal M.P. for Flint Burghs from 1832 to 1837 and for Flintshire from 1837 to 1847. He was also Lord Lieutenant of Flintshire for many years. His contribution to political life was however undistinguished, and he will be remembered principally as Gladstone's brother-in-law, his elder sister having married that redoubtable statesman in 1839. Glynne never married, and on his death in 1874 Hawarden Castle passed to the Gladstone family who still live there.

It is as an antiquarian that Glynne will be remembered. He developed an interest in churches at an early age, and throughout his adult life he spent much time travelling the length and breadth of the country, visiting and making notes on churches. On his death he left notebooks with descriptions of over five and a half thousand churches, carefully organised by county. The descriptions are invaluable because of their accuracy and attention to detail, coupled with the fact that many of his visits took place before the churches were subject to the worst rigours of Victorian restoration.

The notebooks are now in the Clwyd County Record Office in Hawarden. Glynne's descriptions of churches in some counties have been published, but the Hampshire material has remained a virtually unquarried source. He visited Titchfield Church on 10th July 1847, and his description of the church is the only known detailed account of the building before the restoration of 1866-7. He describes the church in the following terms:

"A large Church, constructed of flints, mostly stuccoed — the nave very wide & lofty having a large N. aisle and a somewhat narrower S. aisle. The Chancel spacious & has a large Chantry Chapel on its S. side. At the W. end a plain early Tower without buttresses, but having a 1st Pd. corbel table & small lancets in the belfry story. It is surmounted by a short shingled spire which rises little above the roof of the nave. The lower story of the Tower forms a porch, & within it is a very fine Romanesque doorway, with 3 orders of mouldings, exhibiting rich chevron ornament & shafts with abaci & varied foliage in the capitals. Another Romanesque door remains on the S. side of the nave, of a plainer character with 2 orders of arch mouldings & 1 shaft on each side. The S. aisle is original, though it has undergone some alterations & some late windows have been inserted. Within the original Romanesque arcade on the S. of the nave has been sadly altered of late years in order to make room for the insertion of a gallery — the arches were formerly low, & the piers short, of circular form with square capitals — the arches are now quite changed by 2 being thrown into one — the responds have square abaci with indented ornaments. The North aisle is altogether 3d Pd. of light & good character divided by an arcade of 4 lofty & elegant arches — the piers being light & having each 4 clustered shafts with octagonal capitals. The windows are of 3 lights, except that at the E. — which is of 5 — & had once a reredos under it — of which 2 fine canopied niches still remain, flanking the window & a smaller one in the angle. The nave a great height — the roof externally leaded, internally exhibiting tie beams & struts. The Chancel arch is a plain 1st Pd. one, springing from half circular columns. The Chancel has much of the original Norman wall but the windows on the N. & E. are 3d Pd. — the latter mutilated. The South wall is perforated in its Western portion by 2 curious pointed arches springing from short pillars set upon a very high basement, & apparently of advanced M. Pd work, which is the date of the Chantry. The central pier has 4 clustered shafts each with singularly sculptured capitals representing various monsters & foliage, the bases have round mouldings. Eastwd. of which is the Priests door & 3 fine sedilia of 1st, (verging to M.) Pd. work. The 2 Westward sedilia communicate with each other & have a central detached column of very good character, with responds of the like sort. The Eastward sedile is larger than the others & raised above them — & separate from them but of similar design. At its back appears a large square recess. Eastward of this is a small piscina with trefoil head much mutilated. The East window is flanked by fine 3d Pd niches. The South Chantry is a private burying place, but is spacious & grand — equal in length to the Chancel and with a high pitched tiled roof. It is of M Pd. character, somewhat advanced. The E. window of 3 lights, of a kind not extremely common. The others have each 2 trefoil headed lights, internally contained under an arch but not so within. The E. end is enclosed as a vestry & its boarded partition cuts the sedilia in 2. These are 3 in number, with ogee heads, trefoiled, springing from shafts — & eastward of them is a good piscina having a octofoiled orifice. In the centre of this Chantry (which has a western door) is a large sumptuous tomb of marble, richly painted and gilt to Jane Cts. of Southampton (obt. 1574) whose effigy is raised up very high above the tomb.

The Font is modern, in the Chancel & too small. There are W. and S. galleries in the nave & an upper one at the W. end containing a good organ. In the tower are 4 bells."

In commenting on Glynne's text a few brief words should first of all be devoted to terminology. When Glynne wrote there was no agreed

St Peter's Church Titchfield 1856.

terminology for the three principal periods of Gothic architecture, known to us today as Early English (1180-1290), Decorated (1290-1350) and Perpendicular (1350 to the Reformation). Glynne calls these three periods First Pointed, Middle Pointed and Third Pointed (usually abbreviated to 1st Pd., M.Pd., and 3rd Pd).

The accuracy of Glynne's description of those parts of the church which remain unaltered is noteworthy, as it enables us to place trust in what he says about what has been altered or what has disappeared. A great deal can be learnt from a detailed examination of the text, particularly when taken in conjunction with other surviving sources.

The following points in Glynne's description are particularly worthy of comment:-

(1) Externally the church was mostly rendered. This point is confirmed by another antiquarian, N.W. Deckemant, who visited the church only 2 months after Glynne in September 1847. In a brief note (preserved in the Devon Record Office), Deckemant states that the church 'bears marks of violent plastering and whitewashing.'

(2) The outer walls of the Norman south aisle survived and incorporated a Norman doorway. The existence of this doorway is otherwise unknown; as there was a south porch it does not appear in the various surviving illustrations of the church. It appears that the possibility of re-erecting this doorway in the new aisle built in 1866/7 was considered. Among the faculty papers in the Hampshire Record Office, one plan shows an intention to re-use a doorway corresponding to Glynne's description. Unfortunately this intention was, for some unknown reason, not followed through.

(3) The 'late windows' in the south aisle may be seen in several illustrations. They are square-headed windows of Perpendicular date.

(4) Glynne's description of the arcade of the south aisle confirms other sources which indicate that a single large arch was inserted in place of the two eastern arches of the original Norman arcade, when galleries were inserted in the late eighteenth century (see below). The east end of this arcade may be seen in a painting of the interior of the church which is undated but which is probably to be ascribed to the 1840's and in a photograph dated 1859; both painting and photograph may be seen in the display area in the Southampton Chapel. It remains uncertain whether the original Norman arcade was of 3 or 4 bays before the Georgian alterations.

(5) Glynne is mistaken in stating that the walls of the chancel are of Norman origin. In fact they are of Early English date with inserted windows of the Perpendicular period. His description of the east window as mutilated does however accord well with the evidence of several illustrations, including the painting referred to above. This shows quite clearly that the east window had wooden mullions.

Interior of St Peter's Church c., 1905.

The photograph of 1859 reveals that there was a preliminary restoration of the chancel before the main restoration of 1866/7. By 1859 Perpendicular tracery had been inserted in the east window, with a Gothic reredos below, and there was also a low screen of Gothic design across the chancel-arch. In addition a Gothic-looking organ is to be seen in the eastern bay of the south arcade of the chancel. The date of these works is uncertain, but they must have taken place between Glynne's visit in 1847 and the photograph of 1859. A possible clue is to be found in the *Conspectus of the Diocese of Winchester 1864 by Charles Richard Bishop of Winchester,* which mentions alterations at Titchfield church in 1859, though no details are given. It is indeed possible that the photograph was taken on the occasion of the completion of these works.

(6) Doubt has sometimes been cast over the date of the dwarf wall which supports the arcade on the south side of the chancel, but Glynne's description leaves no doubt that it is an original feature. The wall has undergone later changes; in particular the eastern part has been entirely re-built.

(7) The sedilia and the piscina of the church were much restored in the Victorian period; Glynne's description confirms that the restoration preserved the basic character of their original design.

(8) Glynne's description stresses the character of the Southampton Chapel as a mausoleum. Even today it appears cut off from the rest of the church, and this isolation must have been even more marked when it was only entered from the west through a doorway from the narrow Norman south aisle. The vestry at the east end of the chapel was a recent creation; its construction in 1840 is recorded in the vestry minutes.

(9) The galleries in the south aisle and at the west end of the nave and of the north aisle are well recorded in the documentary sources. At the west end of the nave there was a singing gallery for the choir, known to have been in existence by 1776. The remaining galleries provided reserved seating for middle-class members of the congregation unable to acquire a seat in the main body of the church; most of these galleries appear to have been erected between 1776 and 1801. The low Norman arches of the original south aisle did not provide sufficient headroom, and as noted above, two arches were removed to make way for a single arch. These galleries were anathema to the Victorians and as in many other churches they were swept away when the church underwent restoration.

(10) The upper gallery at the west end is known only from Glynne's description. An organ is first mentioned as having been recently

installed in the church in 1780 and this organ in turn was apparently replaced in 1828. In 1986 removal of plaster from the ringing chamber in the tower revealed traces of a blocked doorway opening at high level towards the nave, and it may be that this doorway was the organist's entrance to his gallery.

It will be evident from these comments that Glynne's account constitutes an invaluable source of information about Titchfield church before restoration, particularly when used in conjunction with other sources. I am much indebted to Sir William Gladstone for permission to reproduce the description here.

REFERENCE:

Original in Clwyd County Record Office.

Michael Hare

REV. G.W.W. MINNS

George Minns was the first serious historian of Titchfield. George William Walter Minns was born at Norwich on 23rd April, 1837. The son of a builder, he was educated at Norwich Grammar School and Cambridge University. Ordained in 1860, he held curacies in Berkshire and Norfolk before spending most of the period from 1863 in France and Italy sketching and studying architecture. He returned to England in 1866, married, and after a variety of positions in Norfolk, Surrey and Middlesex, settled down in 1879 as Vicar of Weston, Southampton. At first, family and parochial commitments kept him fully occupied, but by the late eighties he was able to resume the life-long interest in antiquities which he had had to set aside since leaving Norfolk, and became editor of the Hampshire Field Club *Papers and Proceedings*. In addition to editing wholly or in part the first six volumes of the *Papers and Proceedings*, he assembled the material for the Shore Memorial Volume, carried out a great deal of original research, and published several papers of his own.

Minns carried out excavations at Titchfield Abbey, and published papers on (among other things) "A portrait of Lady Betty Delmé, by Sir Joshua Reynolds formerly at Camms Hall, Fareham with notes on the family of Delmé", "Titchfield Abbey and Place House", "The Catalogue of Titchfield Abbey" and "Remarks on an old map of the ancient parish of Titchfield". This last is of particular importance because both the original map and a full-size tracing commissioned by Minns in connection with his paper have since disappeared; the document is therefore available to us only in the much reduced reproduction published in 1906 as part of Minns' paper. This is the most recent documentary evidence of the original map. However from documents in Hampshire Record Office it would appear that the bulk of Minns' notes and papers were to be sent to Titchfield, with the tracing, in 1920, shortly after Minns' death, and that they were soon afterwards passed to the then Vicar. In 1984 the papers (but not the tracing) appeared at auction and were bought by Hampshire Record Office. Where were they in the meantime, and where is the tracing now? Above all, where is the original?

REFERENCE:

The Titchfield estate from a XVIIth Century Map (Hampshire Field Club.)

Keith Hayward

THE HEWETT FAMILY OF TITCHFIELD

The Hewetts seem to have been in Titchfield in the Middle Ages. A Titchfield Abbey rental of 1377-8 lists a Richard Huyht. In the 1500s the Hewetts were living at Crofton and 200 years later we hear of a John Hewett, who died there in 1746. In his will he mentions "my four closes of land called Crofton Fields and one close called Mitchells, I give and devise to my son James and his heirs according to the custom of the Manor". He also mentions "all my land called Mayles Hollam and 16 acres of land called Cleverleys to my son William". In 1760 Crofton Farm was leased to a John Hewett (presumably the son of James Hewett) by Thomas Bower for £30 a year. In a will dated 1757 he refers to his copyhold messuage and land at Crofton and in a codicil of 1766 he is referred to as a yeoman; by that time he had moved to Posbrook. In fact we hear that in 1762 John Delmé, the Lord of the Manor, had leased to him "all tithe of corn wool and lamb excepting out of the said tithes of corn, yearly and every year one waggon load of wheat and one waggon load of barley such as can be drawn by four horses". John's widow Jane left the contents of Posbrook to her son Robert; he had a son also Robert in 1782.

By the 1851 census we gather that James, who is described as a grandson of John, was living at Posbrook with his children Mary 23, James 20, Elizabeth 18 and six servants. He farmed 700 acres and employed 24 labourers and 7 boys. Great Posbrook was rented (it belonged to the Delmés) but the Hewetts owned Little Posbrook and various other parcels of land.

A James Anderson was living at Hollam in 1789 when he was granted a coat of arms. His great grand-daughter Agnes married James Hewett of Posbrook in 1870. By her marriage settlement she acquired Bridge House, Mill Street, and when James went bankrupt they moved there in 1880. They had three daughters Agnes Elizabeth (Nessie), Mabel Emily (Fluffy) and Edith. The daughters lived together in Bridge House for the rest of their lives. Nessie was known as Farmer Hewett. She had ploughed her fields herself during the First World War. She always wore high laced boots and a longish skirt and jacket — new ones were copied from the old. Fluffy was more modern, had her hair permed and drove a car. She was very concerned with church affairs and was still singing in the choir a few weeks before she died in 1951. Edith did the housekeeping and grew flowers in her greenhouse at Little Posbrook. They are commemorated in a very fine window in the north aisle of the church. Their grandfather Captain James Anderson sold Hollam to Robert Hewett, brother of James Hewett of Posbrook (their great uncle). Robert's grand-daughter

The Misses Hewett; Agnes, Mabel and Edith.

JESUS I HAVE PROMISED TO SERVE THEE TO THE END
Agnes, Mabel and Edith Hewett
loved and served this Church
1872 – 1956

The Hewett memorial window in Titchfield Church.

Rose Greene was the last of the family to live at Hollam which she willed back to her Hewett cousins when she died in 1917.

As well as the three daughters, James and Agnes had three sons. The first was Hewett Brett (Huey). He and his brother Anderson James (Andy) emigrated to New Zealand. John Ridge, the last son, was trained as an electrical engineer, went to the USA and became editor of the *General Electric Review* of the General Electrical Company. Huey had two sons, one of whom married but had no children. John had a daughter Rosemary, who returned to live in Titchfield in 1927. After the death of her last aunt (Edith) in 1956 she had to clear out Bridge House. In the attic were found papers going back to the 1500s, many years of farm account books and sale catalogues from big house sales. The documents are now in the Record Office in Portsmouth. One trunk was full of beautiful Victorian clothes, probably belonging to James' first wife, who died in her first year of marriage. There were also beautifully embroidered sheets 100 years old and other innumerable treasures. Sadly, there are now no Hewetts living in the village.

Rosemary Hewett

FREDERICK BUNNEY

Frederick Bunney was for many years miller at Titchfield Mill, a Parish Councillor and later a Rural District Councillor. We are fortunate to have a sheaf of bills dated 1917-25, which gives us many details of the daily transactions between Mr. Bunney and various tradesmen and shopkeepers around Titchfield. He was a person of some standing, not only the tenant of the mill, but also of Fernhill Farm and the Malthouse in Mill Street. His wife was a daughter of the Fielder family who owned the Brewery. When his house in Catisfield Lane was demolished, these bills were rescued, still on their spike.

The number of shopkeepers and tradesmen contained on this file indicate that Titchfield was still a thriving self-supporting community, supplying practically everything for the needs of its inhabitants. Mr West of High Street, one of a number of butchers in the town, supplied beef, sirloin and steak — delivered by an errand boy. Drapery including underwear for his wife came from Thorolds, East Street. We find on the bill from Johnsons, a High Street baker, that a lard cake price 4d was delivered every Saturday with payment anything up to six weeks later! A bill made out by J.G. Hack, a Sarisbury Green butcher, who also supplied Mr Bunney, tells us that meat supplied between November 1916 and April 1917 totalled 15s. 4½p; it was not settled until the following August. Another bill is headed "W. Bannister and Sons (September 13th 1918) Ladies' and Gents' Tailors and Outfitters. Liveries and Breeches. Costumes a Speciality". Livery tailors supplied the uniforms for the servants of the rich families; each had their own button pattern which the tailor used when making suits for his clients. In September 1918 Bannister's received an order for a grey ulster at £4. 4s. to be fitted with a fur collar at £1. 1s. with 2s. 6d. extra for sewing it on. The bill for the coat was unusually paid within two weeks. Mr. Hackett did quite a lot of work for Mr. Bunney at his house, Dingley Dell, in Swanwick. Two items dated February-March 1917, thawing frozen pipes and repairing three bursts in pipes, indicate a severe winter. Mr. Hackett had a telephone number: tel. 13 Locksheath. Hugh Swinstead, Nurseyman, Swanwick, supplied fruit trees four years old at 5s. each: apples in the following varieties — Gladstone, Wealthy, Newton Wonder: pear — Doyenne du Comice: plums — Czar and Victoria at 4s.

Mr. Bunney's mill must have been a substantial concern, as we see from a bill for wheat supplied by R.S. Mortimer in 1918, between May 2nd and May 22nd: during this period 360 qrs were received. The cost was £1,383 8s. 4½d of which Mr. Bunney paid £1,000 on June 3rd and the balance two weeks later. As usual Mr. Bunney deducted

The Village from the air in the 1950's.

something for short weight, 18s. 6d on this occasion. Frederick Bunney made many vigorous contributions to public debate. In November 1919 for instance when the Parish Council was discussing the provision of postal addresses, he spoke at the meeting saying that personally he was against ... "Titchfield had done without the numbering of houses for hundreds of years".

Trevor Cox

THE PARISH COUNCIL

Between 1894 and 1932 Titchfield had its own parish council. Elected parish councils were brought into existence by Act of Parliament to create a bottom tier of democratic government, and to take over some of the roles which the old vestry meetings had exercised for hundreds of years. In the process the ancient parish was split up, and separate parish councils created for Crofton, Sarisbury and Hook-with-Warsash, in addition to Titchfield itself. But after less than 40 years the national politicians changed their minds, and many of the parish councils were abolished, to be merged within the larger District authorities. The four Titchfield civil parishes disappeared for ever into the Fareham District. But in the four decades of their existence they provided an important focus for the energies of their citizens, and in their minute books they have left us with fascinating evidence of the half-forgotten concerns of our grandparents.

One of these concerns in Titchfield was public order. Titchfield had (and to some extent still has) a reputation as a 'rough' village. It is doubtful, in fact, whether Titchfield has ever been very different from any of hundreds of historic English communities in which long-

A school outing at the 'Rec' c., 1925 with Headmaster Mr Upshall (left) and 'Josher' Williams.

established social patterns have not always been consistent with more modern notions of civilised behaviour. But there is no doubt that Titchfield Parish Council, throughout its history, was concerned about unruly behaviour and vandalism. One focus of such concern was the then new Recreation Ground, established to mark Queen Victoria's Jubilee in 1897. The 'Rec.' took on something of the role in Titchfield life that was taken by the urinal in the fictional French village of Clochemerle. That the councillors futily ordered 'unclimbable' fencing for the Rec. shows that they had anticipated the events which were to follow. From the day it opened, the turf, fences, gates and later pavilion, urinal and children's swings were persistently vandalised. In 1911 the council discussed the unruly conduct of the boys on the recreation ground: it was reported that "the conduct of some of the bigger boys was very bad". The caretaker could not keep order when games were being played. The problem was still going on in 1920 when the boys were said to be "interfering in games and making themselves offensive". Bad behaviour was one factor in the vexed question of the Sunday opening of the Rec., which was a bitterly fought out dispute in the early 1920s. At the same time another bitter dispute was taking place between the village Football Club and the village Cricket Club on the use of the ground. There was no

Titchfield's football team.

room for a separate cricket square, and the footballers damaged the lovingly prepared pitch. In the end it was the footballers who won.

Other public assets for which many villagers showed little respect were the cemeteries — the old graveyard at the parish church, and from 1916 onwards the new cemetery in Posbrook Lane. Once again, the gates and fences were regularly damaged, and flowers and vases taken from graves. When barbed wire was put along the tops of fences to stop the boys climbing over, small girls were reported to have squeezed themselves underneath. In 1919 it was reported that the graves of two distinguished and recently deceased parishioners, General Gordon and Frederick Bunney, had both been damaged.

Bad behaviour was not confined to the recreation ground and the cemeteries. In October 1899 there were complaints about behaviour in the village itself, and in the following January it was said that "there did not appear to be any considerable alteration in the unruly behaviour in the streets in the evening": the police constable should spend more time in the village. But things did not improve. In 1923 there were complaints about the obstruction caused by men and youths standing about on street corners; and a fracas in the Square in 1927 was the occasion for a Mr. Goddard to be presented with a silver watch for the assistance he had given to the constable. The gypsies who came into the parish during the strawberry season were seen as one cause of the trouble: but in the summer of 1927 the trouble was blamed on "a rough element of the Air Force at Lee". It would appear that the 1920s were no more the Good Old Days than the 1820s had been.

A rather different problem which exercised the Titchfield Parish Council in those years was the impact of the internal combustion engine. It first came to the councillors' attention early in 1904 when as a result of the Motor Car Act of 1903 they were required to put up notices at dangerous places in the village. The inadequate state of the roads was discussed in 1909 and it was agreed to ask the County Council to use 'hard metal' for the road surfaces: one very up-to-date councillor (J.R. Fielder) suggested that the streets should be sprayed with tar. The possibility of a bus service was first mentioned in March 1920, when councillor Walter Smith suggested that "a service of motors from Portsmouth to Southampton calling and picking up at all the intervening villages would be very beneficial to the public at large". Councillor George Powell spoke against the idea: "he seemed a bit doubtful as to whether the scheme would pay" (George Powell ran a horse-drawn carrier service). By September 1922 the problems were mounting. There were complaints about fast motor traffic and excessive speeds, especially at the very dangerous corners of Southampton Hill and the High Street, and Coach Hill and South Street. Portsmouth United Brewery's lorry was causing an obstruction when unloading outside the Coach and Horses, and Lankester and Crook's delivery van was driving too fast down West Street. It was suggested that a 5 m.p.h. speed limit should be imposed in the village, and warning notices put up. A year later it was reported that the District Council were considering buying and demolishing the cottage which then stood at the corner of Southampton Hill and East Street. By early in 1924 the motor buses which George Powell had opposed were racing in competition through the streets, just as the stage-coaches had done a century before: now it was the 'Enterprise' against the Southdown Motor Company. The Parish Council appealed to the Automobile Association for more warning signs, but in 1926 an A.A. inspector advised that in his opinion "Drive Slowly notices have no effect on the average motorist". Titchfield had moved into yet another new era. By the end of the 1920s there was a by-pass between the village and the Recreation Ground, by 1978 an eastern by-pass, and by 1980 a motorway through the north of the ancient parish.

Quite a different topic on which the Parish Council minutes cast light is the painfully slow emancipation of women. The democracy which the Parish Council represented in 1894 was democracy for men. Women were almost never heard of in discussions in the 1890s. The Queen, of course, was occasionally mentioned. The death of Mrs White, the Vicar's wife, was noted with respect in 1896. A Ladies Committee helped to run the 1897 festivities. When money was being raised for the new recreation ground, the council wrote to Miss Greene (Rose E. Greene) at Sackville House, Piccadilly, described as the second biggest landowner in the district, to ask if she would pay for the shelter there: she refused, though she later sent £5. The key to the churchyard was kept at Mrs Gough's house; and condolences were sent to Mrs Gladstone on her husband's death. That was the sum total of references to the other sex in the councillors' deliberations before 1900.

It was the First World War that transformed the situation. In August 1914 the Vicar, the Reverend C.E. Matthews, the council chairman, was called up, and Mrs. Matthews was designated to receive cheques on his behalf. In November, Mrs. R.H. Tremlett was elected to be a collector of the special expenses rate. In December 1916, at a meeting to discuss War Savings, a Mrs. Conway spoke, and Mrs. Bernard Davis and Miss D. Ings were elected to the committee. The year 1917 saw further developments. The part-time parish clerk (Leslie Carden) was called up, and the council agreed to accept applications from women as well as men. There were three applications — from the school headmaster, Mr. Upshall, from Leslie's sister Miss Carden, and from Miss Fearne. Mr. Upshall got the job — by one vote from Miss Carden. A few months' later, Miss Carden's name appears as the only woman attending a public meeting. By this time too, the Postmistress was Miss Walker. The most dramatic year was 1919. Older women now had the vote, and four women were present at the annual parish meeting in March — two of the Misses Hewitt, Mrs Matthews (the Vicar's wife) and Mrs Mason (the chemist's wife). Miss Agnes Hewitt was nominated — and elected! — to the Parish Council, shortly afterwards joining the Allotments Committee and speaking on agricultural matters. The Misses Hewitt were also present at a parish meeting to discuss the sewerage issue in 1921, in the company of Miss Parr of St. Margaret's Priory. By 1922 there was a Women's Constitutional Club in the village, with Agnes Hewitt as chairman, which took a vigorous part in the arguments about the Sunday opening of the recreation ground and which campaigned for a village tennis club. In 1929 Agnes Hewitt was offered the vice-chairmanship of the Parish Council, but she declined. Agnes Hewitt was a remarkable woman, but she remained something of an exception to the unspoken rules. It was to take another war before Titchfield women were regularly to find themselves in the chair of any organisations that were not exclusively for women.

These have been only three of the topics on which the minutes of the Parish Council shed light: there are many others that deserve research — the provision of sewerage and piped water, education, council housing, footpaths, the Gas Company, the Fire Brigade, the abortive railway station scheme and so on. We must be grateful to those part-time parish clerks who entered up their minute books in such entertaining detail.

REFERENCE:

Titchfield Parish Council Minutes, Hampshire Record Office, 37M73A, PX1-9

George Watts

A TITCHFIELD GIRLHOOD

Older Girls' class at the National School 1920-21.

I was born in Titchfield, in the Old Inn House in West Street, and grew up there in the 1920s. In those days very few of the houses belonged to the occupiers. In the 1930s they were let for 5s. a week or less, with 2s. for rates, and some were still thatched (three in West Street where the sarsens stand). Many of the people were poor — some just made a living by going down to Meon shore to collect and sell cockles and whelks. For some the Earl of Southampton's Charity provided a £10 grocery ticket at Christmas which had to be spent in one of the shops in the village. The charity also supported local lads as apprentices to local firms such as Freemantles and gave them £20 to buy tools (they were paid 3s. 6d. a week). Many of the girls went into domestic service, but there was also employment in a laundry at Locksheath and later a jam factory on the Common specialising in strawberry jam, the fruit being collected from the allotments in the area. Many of the people in the village worked in the tannery.(J. Watkins and Co.) which remained in business until the 1950s.

There were far more shops in the village than there are now. The largest grocers was Lankester and Crooks at the corner of the Square and West Street. I can well remember the mingled smell of bacon, paraffin,

Church St c., 1920.

meat and groceries of all kinds. There were several more small grocers — two facing each other in West Street. The Bungey family had a tailor's shop in the High Street, and a saddler's shop at the corner of the Square and Church Street. William Bungey in Coach Hill was a decorator. There were two butchers. One was in the High Street (opposite the Parish Room). This is now a private house but the building which was the slaughter house is still next door. Colliholes in the Square was a draper's shop. After the strawberry season many little girls were bought new frocks which they sometimes had "on approval". There was a milliner called Thorolds in East Street. On the ground floor of what is now Bettons was a cycle shop where the owner would make up a bicycle from second-hand parts for 5s. Mr. Williams (Oily Willy) was a lamp and oil dealer in premises next to Bettons in South Street. The mill was still operating as a mill, Mr. Russell then being the miller. There were two shoe shops, one in the house on the left at the end of Mill Street, and another in South Street, run by Alice Monday, a very old lady who never

East Street showing 'Peppernose' Cross's Antique shop on right.

seemed to collect the money owed to her for shoes. There were eight licensed premises. Behind one, the Red House in South Street, a marquee was erected once a year where Joe Beckett, a boxer, took on all comers; moving pictures were also shown there, with tickets at 1d.

Until the coming of Tuck's buses the only way into Fareham was by carrier cart which went once a day and cost 6d. I can still remember walking into Fareham to pay 3d for a seat in the pictures and a penny for a bun afterwards. If transport was needed to the station a horse-drawn victoria could be hired from the Bugle for 2s. 6d. Doctors charged 2s. 6d. for a visit, but if the children had bad whooping cough the mothers sometimes wheeled them down to Hillhead where there was a flock of sheep, believing that being among the sheep would cure them. Choir outings to Lee on the Solent were by farm cart. Until the late 1920s all the road traffic came through the village, and I can remember in the First World War soldiers with bands marching up Southampton Hill on their way to the docks. During the strawberry season large numbers of gypsies came into the district. They sold horses in the Square and bought cheap meat from the butchers. On those occasions two policemen were on duty in the Square in case of trouble. In 1918 the Kaiser was burnt in effigy in the Square as well as the traditional tar barrels which did not improve the paintwork of the houses. The National School was in West Street, but

'Oily' Williams' shop, South Street c., 1938.

there was also a Manse school for the under fives in what is now the Day Rooms, for which the Minister charged 1d. a week. Lord and Lady Hotham then lived at West Hill House. They had a coach and footmen and their invalid daughter was taken to church in a bath-chair.

People used nicknames in those days. As well as "Oily" Williams and "Josher" Williams, I can remember "Peppernose" Cross, "Farm" Hewett, "Hoppy" Ford, "Suety" Waters, the "Whistling Baker" (George Read), and many others.

May Watts

Titchfield Fête Baby Show 1921.

TITCHFIELD CHARITIES

TITCHFIELD WELFARE TRUST (EARL OF SOUTHAMPTON TRUST)

The Titchfield Welfare Trust is founded on a Charity Scheme sealed on 3rd February 1969. This legal document states the aims and the rules governing the conduct of the Charity's affairs. At the same time two relatively modern charities, the Seymour Robert Delmé and the Charlotte Hornby charities (founded in 1894 and 1890 respectively) were merged with three much older charities which had already been amalgamated in 1897. These three charities date back 200-300 years.

Robert Godfreys Charity

A copy of an indenture dated 1597 reveals that in the eighteenth year of Elizabeth I (1576) Robert Godfrey bought a little overwood and close at Funtley from Peter Osborne. Robert Godfrey in his lifetime "had a good and charitable intent and meaning that the whole benefit and commodity of the said wood and close should be employed towards and for the relief of the poor of the town of Titchfield". Although this intent was apparently contained in his Will, the conveyance of the property had not been so amended in his lifetime and so on his death passed to his lawful heir and niece, Anne Croucher.

In 1597 therefore eight inhabitants of the Parish "knowing the good intent of the said Robert Godfrey toward the poor people and being willing to further the same, disbursed twenty pounds of lawful money of England to Stephen and Anne Croucher" for this land eventually to be called "Lavy's Farm".

The income from the property was paid to the Churchwardens of the Parish of Titchfield to "distribute and bestow the same with the consent of the greatest part of the inhabitants of the town of Titchfield to the poor people". The annual income of about £20 was distributed amongst the poor widows, each being allowed 2s. 6d. (12½p), and other persons in sums varying from £1 to 1s. From several Indentures dated between 1723 and 1874 the succession of the Trustees can be traced. Rent was collected from Lavy's Farm regularly at Michaelmas and distributed on 21st December each year. The records of the disbursement of the Charity throughout the eighteenth and nineteenth centuries still exist, although inspection of them is not very rewarding as only the names of the recipients and the amount given are recorded.

Earl of Southampton's Charity

An indenture dated 18th May 1620 between Henry, the third Earl of Southampton and Arthur Bromfield, Robert Churcher and sixteen other inhabitants of the town of Titchfield, recited that: "The town of Titchfield was of late much decayed and impoverished for want of trade, and that being situated near the sea coast, it was a very fit place for the making of woollen cloth, or some other good trade. The Earl of Southampton in consideration of the love he bore to the said town and to the intent that trade might be renewed and continued there, and the poor people of the said town set to work" granted to the Trustees for the term of 500 years:

a messuage, barn, outhouse, orchard and garden and two closes adjoining thereto of approximately 5 acres (Barry's cottages and meadow)

a little close adjoining the churchyard of approximately 1 acre (now part of the churchyard).

a close of 1 acre in Gaston Land (Garston)

Pound Purrock, 1 acre and two cottages in the park (adjacent to Hunts Pond Road).

In 1738 the Churchwardens and Overseers of the Poor of Titchfield filed a petition in the Court of Chancery against William Churcher, the descendant of Robert Churcher, who was believed to be the last survivor of the Trustees of the deed of 1620. It was stated that "the woollen trade had been lost to Titchfield, principally in consequence of the channel which had been navigable to the sea having become diverted from the town and it was prayed that the defendant might be decreed to apply the trust premises to the relief of the poor, or some other charitable use agreeable to the donor's intent". It took fifteen years, however until 1st September 1753, before an indenture between Peter Delmé, Richard Vear (the great grandson of Robert Churcher) and eight Trustees legally re-established the Charity. Accounts and minutes exist for this charity from that time.

Godwin's Gift

Richard Godwin by a will of 1703, charged his lands in the parish of St. Johns in Glastonbury (called Pressmores) with an annual rent charge of £4 to be paid to the Overseers of the Poor and Churchwardens of Titchfield, to be employed by them in teaching twelve poor children to read the English tongue by some lawful Protestant schoolmaster or schoolmistress. This rent is paid to this day.

The Seymour Robert Delmé and Charlotte Hornby Charities

Both these charities bequeathed sums of money to be invested to provide an income for the relief of the poor of Titchfield. The details of the Delmé gift can be seen on a plaque just inside the Church door. The income in this case was used to provide vouchers for the purchase of groceries by poor people. The income from the Hornby charity was used to provide coal for the old people each alternate year. Both incomes have now been swamped by inflation, but the original bequests still form part of the Trust's main investment.

Charitable Acivities in Titchfield Since the Mid-Eighteenth Century

The records of the Earl of Southampton's Charity are reasonably detailed and continuous since 1750. As it is also the major charity it therefore provides a good picture of the part played by charities in Titchfield over the last 200 years.

In 1752 the land re-acquired for the charity was leased to Mr. Thomas Knight to provide an income, and a Mr. John Greenvill was appointed to manage the Charity and to carry on the trade of spinning worsted. He was supported by Dame Hart who taught the poor children spinning, knitting and reading. A minute of 1761 is worthy of note:

> "At a meeting of the Trustees of the Earl of Southampton's Charity, 'tis ordered that the children from the Workhouse in Titchfield in the winter season shall be at the Knitting House at 8 o'clock in the

morning, go home to dinner at 12 o'clock, return at one o'clock and leave at 4 o'clock and in the summer season to be there at 7 o'clock in the morning, go home to dinner at 11 o'clock, return at one o'clock and leave off work at 5 o'clock".

By 1777 the spinning venture had failed, which in retrospect is not surprising since spinning was one of the first trades to be mechanised in the Industrial Revolution. There is no further mention of the Spinning Master in the records. Dame Hart, however, was retained to teach the poor children. She was to become the first in a line of five schoolmistresses to be employed by the Charity until the National School was built in 1830 on part of Barry's Meadow. Distribution of the Charity initially took the form of grants of money to tradesmen who found themselves in difficulties. Shoemakers and cordwainers seemed particularly vulnerable in the mid eighteenth century although most other trades seem to be represented. It is interesting to note that there were at least three impecunious peruke (wig) makers in Titchfield at that time. The Charity also supported other worthy needs:

"7th November 1757 — James Suatt paid £10.10s.0d. to enable him to pay for his wife learning the art of mid-wifery".

From 1790 onwards there was a noticeable change in the type of charitable support given. Throughout the five year period 1790-1795 the aged, sick, widowed, poor and distressed families began to dominate the individual charitable grants. At the same time a Poor Rate was also levied on the Charity between 1794 and 1807. Another important change occured:

"23rd January 1795 — ordered on account of the severe weather ...to be given 2 chaldrons of coal a week for three weeks to the poor inhabitants of the town of Titchfield".

The distribution of goods rather than direct grants was to continue until the Poor Law Amendment Act of 1834. In August 1795 bread was also distributed to the poor. During the inflationary period 1810-1816 the amount of coal distributed was increased — a very sensible way of helping the poor in a period of higher prices. When by 1818 the coal prices had returned to pre-war levels both bread and meat were distributed and in 1820s clothing (40 flannel waistcoats, 40 flannel petticoats and 95 pairs of stockings) and blankets were distributed

From the records of the Charity therefore it appears that, in Titchfield at least in the early nineteenth century an adaptive social security system of sorts existed. The Poor Law Amendment Act of 1834 therefore seems to have been inappropriate in Titchfield and certainly confused the Trustees:

"At a meeting of the Trustees of this Charity held on 2nd February

1836 at the Bugle Inn it was resolved that the distribution of the funds of this Charity be suspended for the present to give time to enquire if the trustees are justified in applying it as heretofore and that meantime the funds be invested in the Fareham Savings Bank".

The answer to the Trustees' enquiry reflects the attitude towards the poor at that time:

"A meeting this 12 day April 1836. The Trustees of this Charity having applied to the Commissioners of Charities and received their answer as to the disposal of the funds of this Charity are of the opinion that they cannot be laid out more in accordance with the will of the donor. Resolve that a majority of the Trustees shall be able to vote such small sums of money as shall seem to them fit to assist tradesmen in need as heretofore but at the same time feel themselves called upon to express in the minutes of their proceedings their intention to promote the habits of industry among the poor by every means in their power".

Poor rates were recommenced in 1839, and although the Charity no longer made a direct distribution of goods to the poor, regular contributions were made to a clothing club and to a coal fund. Grants to tradesmen were increased and in 1840 the first apprenticeship was supported. Nevertheless with less expenditure money began to accumulate.

The Charity purchased Skinhouse in 1842 following a series of disputes concerning encroachment of buildings from Skinhouse on to the Churchyard Meadow. In 1859, however, Churchyard Meadow was sold to the Burial Board to form what is now the lower half of the Churchyard. The money obtained was used to purchase 14½ acres of newly enclosed land adjoining the Charity's land at Hunts Pond Road. The whole was referred to as 'Southfields'. It was decided to demolish the buildings at Skinhouse and to use the materials to build facilities at Southfields. In 1864 the Pest House and more land adjoining Southfields were purchased and a barn, cattle shed and a stable erected there. The sale of these properties one hundred years later has provided the bulk of the Charity's current investment.

The first Charity Scheme of 1897 not only combined the three charities outlined but also, for the first time, laid down specific rules for the conduct of the newly constituted Charity's affairs. With typical Victorian thoroughness the income was to be divided into 23 parts. 18 parts were to be used by an Industrial Branch and 5 parts by an Eleemosynary Branch: the former being in support of apprenticeships, technical instruction, purchase of tools and the like, the latter being in support of the poor with direct charitable grants, pensions, supply of coal or clothing, nursing for the sick, infirm and so on.

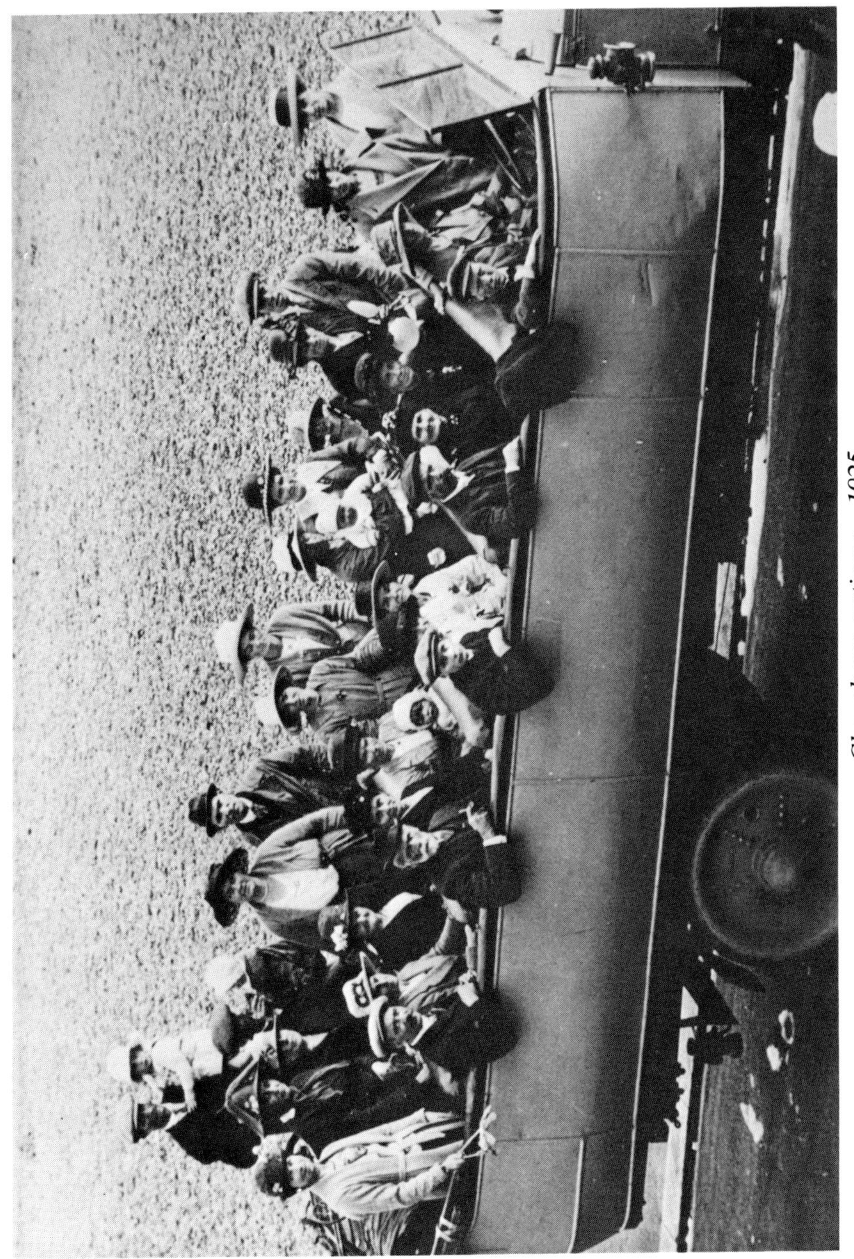

Charabanc outing c., 1925.

This division of the Charity's expenditure by the Charity Commissioners was disliked by the Trustees who believed that the disbursement of the funds should be left to them, or at the very least that the proportions should have been the other way around. At first the Trustees appeared to be justified; apprentices were slow in coming forward for sponsorship in spite of advertisement. As soon as the Charity Commissioners rescinded the order in 1902, however, the apprentice scheme caught on, and up until World War I anything between three and six apprentices were supported each year. Pensions were paid to the elderly poor who were not in receipt of Poor Relief. Contributions were made to a Clothing Club and between 1910 and 1915 to a Parish Nurse Fund. In 1907 an Education Foundation was set up within the Charity in which £4 per year was used for prizes in the local National Schools (Godwin's Gift) and £10 per year to support technical education.

Much of the Charity's business following 1897, however, was dominated by the administration of what was by now a significant estate. Southfields had been split into 17 allotments in 1892 to obtain a larger income, but it is clear that many of the tenants were canny folk. The Rent Collector did not have an easy job!

The First World War not only caused a dearth of apprentices but saw the Chairman sent off to France and when the Clerk was called up; for the first time a lady was appointed as Clerk to the Trustees, Miss Carden. As a result of the neglect of the Charity's property throughout the war followed by rising prices in the immediate post war period, the Charity came under financial strain. Between 1919 and 1921 no pensions could be paid, rents were increased for the allotments but had to be reduced in the bad seasons of 1925-27. By 1938 many of the allotments were reported derelict and appear to have remained that way until they were taken over and ploughed up by the War Agricultural Committee in 1941. The old National School building underwent a similar decline. Having reverted to the Charity in 1933 it was not until 1937 that part was let to the Boxing Club, and in 1938 part to the Titchfield Boys Club. In 1942 it was requisitioned by the military and although in 1944 American Troops were reported to be generally tidying it up, when it was de-requisitioned in 1945 it was reported to be almost derelict.

Altogether, by the end of the Second World War the Charity's property was in a very poor state. Lavy's Farmhouse and the Pest House both required major works and the Lock Up (the old Market Hall) which appears to have been moved on to Barry's Meadow in 1845 by the Lord of the Manor, was in a dangerous state. With little chance of increasing income by increasing rents and in keeping with the Charity Commissioners' policy at the time, Lavy's Farm, the Pest House, Garstons Garden, the gardens to Barry's Cottages and parts of Barry's

St Peter's choir with Vicar Spurway c., 1947.

Meadow were sold and the money invested.

A new Charity Scheme was sealed in 1969 which renamed the Charity as the Titchfield Welfare Trust and changed the emphasis to Relief in Need but only in areas not covered by the Social Services. The sale of Southfields to Hampshire County Council in 1977 has reversed the Trust's fortunes and opened a new era in its history. The Trust is currently (1989) increasing its number of almshouses, and the Charity Scheme is being amended accordingly. In future the Charity is to be generally known as The Earl of Southampton Trust.

D.G. Smith

Residents of Titchfield with their Best Kept Village in Hampshire Award 1988.

Titchfield in the 1980s

At the end of *Titchfield: A History,* published in 1982, we commented on the tide of houses and factories sweeping over many parts of the ancient parish. That process has continued throughout the decade. Brick, tile and tarmac have rolled over the arable fields west of Stubbington and Crofton, over the old strawberry holdings on Titchfield Common, and over the former hunting chase of Titchfield Park (which has now confusingly borrowed the name of Segensworth). In particular, the wave of development has broken over the line of the motorway and crashed into the beautiful, historic and once secluded area of Whiteley. The closure of the Swanwick Basket Factory has been one consequence of these changes. Closer to the village, the impending arrival of Raychem on the Kite's Croft site will have a particularly important impact on the local scene. Within the village itself, the 1980s have seen several years of lively controversy over the proposed sale of the Vicarage and the construction of new "Chapter Rooms" partly inside the fabric of the famous church. More positively, the village has won the best kept Hampshire village award in the successive years 1987 and 1988. Clubs and societies of all kinds flourish. Bonfire Day has continued to be a major event in south Hampshire. The recreation and conservation areas fringing the coast have been preserved and improved. A new museum at Fareham will make our rich heritage much better known. It has been the deep historic roots of Titchfield and of the other old communities within the boundaries of the ancient parish which has enabled them to resist the homogenising and depersonalising effects of suburban sprawl. We expect that resistance to continue.

George Watts

Further reading

A number of important background books were listed at the end of *Titchfield: A History,* 1982. This note will mention some useful books published since then. *The Portsmouth Region* ed. B. Stapleton and J.H. Thomas (Alan Sutton, 1989) puts Titchfield in the context of south-east Hampshire. *The Place-Names of Hampshire,* Richard Coates (Batsford, 1989) gives authoritative interpretations of the major place-names in the parish. *Domesday Book: Hampshire* ed. J.Munby (Phillimore, 1982) is a new translation in a convenient format. *The Industrial Heritage of Hampshire and the Isle of Wight,* P. Moore (Phillimore, 1988) is the most recent treatment of its subject. There are many references to medieval Titchfield in *The Register of William Edington Bishop of Winchester* Parts 1 and 2 ed. S.F. Hockey (Hampshire County Council, 1987). Some interesting medieval material, particularly on Crofton, is in *The Cartularies of Southwick Priory* ed. K.A. Hanna (Hampshire County Council, 1988). *Hampshire and the Isle of Wight* (Ordnance Survey Historical Guides, 1988) reproduces one of the versions of the early one-inch map. F.W. Light's *Short History of Warsash* was reprinted by Spotlight Magazine in 1986. The *Proceedings of the Hampshire Field Club* 39 (1983) contained "Peasant Discontent on the Manors of Titchfield Abbey", D.G. Watts. The same publication, volume 40 (1984) contained "The Watergate at Portchester and the Anglo-Saxon Porch at Titchfield", M. Hare. The Hampshire Field Club has also republished *The Titchfield estate from a XVIIth Century Map* (the 1610 map), first published in 1894, the original of which is now lost. *Fareham: Past and Present* ed. A James has regularly published articles on features of Titchfield ancient parish. The Stubbington W.E.A. Local History Group has published *A Look at Stubbington 1850-1875* (1984) and *Life in late seventeenth Stubbington* (1986). Titchfield History Society itself has published John Achard's plan of Place House or Titchfield House of 1737; *The Hearth Tax Return for the Hundred of Titchfield* (1985); and regular issues of its newsletter *The Titchfield Historian.*

Acknowledgements
The Titchfield History Society would like to thank all the contributors of articles and all the people who loaned photographs for inclusion in this volume. The editorial committee has been Vernon Belding, Trevor Cox, Keith Dingle, Keith Hayward, Richard Wade, George Watts and Sally Wise. Keith Dingle has prepared the photographs and Vernon Belding the drawings and maps. Richard Wade has prepared the index. The illustrations have been arranged by Vernon Belding and Sally Wise. We are grateful for the permission of the editor of *Fareham: Past and Present* to use the articles on 'Titchfield Abbey Library' and 'Some Parish records' first published in that journal. We acknowledge particularly the extensive use made in this volume of material from the Hampshire Record Office in Winchester. Finally, our grateful thanks to the typists, Mrs. Arnett and Mrs. Herrick.

The Knife Grinder in Gardner Road 1968.

INDEX
(a select index of people and places)

Great Abshot 27,80
Amoore & Sons 82
James Anderson 80,96
J. Ashburnham 38
W. Bannister & Sons 100
Bishop's Sutton 38
The Breach 25
Lord Brook 51,53
Arthur Broomfield 46
Mary Brown 32
Brownwich Manor 25,80
The Bungey family 80,85,109
Cams Hall 85
Mr. Chamberlain 46
Churchyard meadow 116
The Coach & Horses 83
Colliholes 109
Crofton 96,103
Sir T. Danvers 36
The Delmé family 80,96,112,114
T. Dymock 36
Fairs 80
Fernhill Farm 100
Fleet End 23
W. Franklin 82
Fontley 15
Fontley Iron Mill 46
The Fryer family 79
Earl of Gainsborough 51
John de Gisors 10
Robert Godfrey 112
Richard Godwin 114
General Gordon 84
George Gough 82
Sir S. Glynn 87
J. Grove 82
Mr. Hackett 100
Col. Hammond 38
Hartwells 46
Sir T. Heneage 35
The Hewett family 80,85,96
Hillhead 25
Hook 80
John Hornby 80
Hound 56
Hubbard's Mill 79
Edward Ives 74
Edward Otto Ives 74
John Jermayne 44
Kite's Croft 7
Lankester & Crook 108
J. Leaton 82
Locks Heath 108
H. Long 36
The market 80,85
The Rev. C.E. Matthews 106
The Rev. G.W.W. Minns 95
The Missings 65,82
Jesse Mitchell 82
E. & T. Monday 82
Mr. Newsham 53
The Oglanders 29
William de Pageham 13
Park Farm 22
Pest House 116
Posbrook 96
Duke of Portland 52
Elizabeth Privett 63
Queen's Head 83
Recreation Ground 104
Peter de Roches 11
Rowner 56

Sabyns 46
Sarisbury 100
Schools 110,118
Segensworth Farm 80
1st Earl of Southampton 24
3rd Earl of Southampton 32,46,113
4th Earl of Southampton 38
4th Earl's daughters 40
Southampton House 40
J. Suatt 82
Swanwick 7
The Tannery 108
H. Tapper 82
Admiral Thompson 83
Thorolds 100
The Rev. Wm. Thresher 80
Titchfield Park Farm 80
Stephen de Turnham 10
Mr. Upshall 106
Clement Walcott 24
Warsash 82

Place House from the North-East (see page 51).